GREAT BEERS
of the World

AND HOW TO BREW THEM AT HOME

Also by the same author:

The Complete Guide to Home Brewing in Australia

GREAT BEERS
of the World

AND HOW TO BREW THEM AT HOME

LAURIE STRACHAN

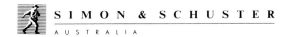
SIMON & SCHUSTER
AUSTRALIA

GREAT BEERS OF THE WORLD AND HOW TO BREW THEM AT HOME

First published in Australia in 2000 by
Simon & Schuster (Australia) Pty Limited
20 Barcoo Street, East Roseville NSW 2069

A Viacom Company
Sydney New York London Toronto Tokyo Singapore

National Library of Australia
Cataloguing-in-Publication data:

Strachan, Laurie.
Great beers of the world and how to brew them at home.

Bibliography.
Includes index.
ISBN 0 7318 0762 6.
1. Beer. 2. Beer-History. 3. Brewing. I. Title.
641.23

Cover design: Gaynor Murphy, Greendot Design
Internal design: DiZign

Set in Rotis Serif
Printed in China by Everbest

10 9 8 7 6 5 4 3 2 1

Dedication

To Jenny and Fyfe for never complaining
about the clutter, the cursing and the
pervasive smell of brewing in their home.

Contents

Foreword

Beer is the single most popular drink in the world—and its origins go well back in history. Every nation brews and enjoys beer, and every nation has its own beer styles. However, few beer drinkers are aware of the great variety of high-quality beers available across the world.

It has been my pleasure and good fortune over the past 28 years to be involved in the brewing of some of these beers in America, Australia, New Zealand and Asia—and I never tire of tasting new styles and varieties. I have found that beer, being lower in alcohol than wines and spirits, offers beneficial health effects when consumed in moderation. In addition, it is a beverage of refreshment well suited to complementing a good meal.

Laurie Strachan's excellent book is an encouragement to drink in moderation. It stresses the rich character of beer—rather than its effects; the pleasure to be gained from savouring the flavour—rather than the dubious effects of drinking to excess. Simply stated, this book stresses quality over quantity.

In *Great Beers of the World and How to Brew Them at Home*, Laurie has comprehensively surveyed and analysed the world's great beer styles. He has investigated how they originated, why they have been enduringly popular, and why they have their particular characteristics. But he has gone even further, and has carefully analysed the brewing techniques that we brewers have developed over the years to make our beers more healthy, better tasting and more satisfying. His detailed brewing descriptions may even tempt discerning beer connoisseurs to try brewing for themselves.

This book will help to increase everyone's knowledge of one of life's great pleasures. I recommend it heartily.

Dr Charles (Chuck) Hahn
Director and Brewmaster
Hahn Brewery and Malt Shovel Brewery
Sydney
April 2000

Preface

It is possible to develop an interest in, even a love of, beer—without knowing anything much about how it is made. However, as with most interests, greater knowledge usually brings greater enjoyment. For a wine buff, the ability to detect what grape variety has been used in the vintage, and where and when the wine was made, is basic to enhancing the pleasure of drinking. The same should be true of beer, but it seldom is. One of the reasons is that many of the most popular texts on beer appreciation touch only lightly on the processes by which beer is made—and without a basic grasp of these processes, it is difficult to really understand how and why one beer differs from another, other than in the most obvious ways.

This book aims to bridge the gap between drinker and brewer by showing how the myriad beer styles of the world have evolved, and how the drinker who wishes to delve further into the world of beer can do so in the most revealing way—by brewing beer himself or herself (for beer and brewing are by no means exclusively male domains).

The art and science of brewing is therefore the theme that unites the various sections of this book. The book deals first with the history and evolution of beer. It then moves onto a description of beer styles. Finally, the book deals with the techniques used in making beer, and concludes with a series of recipes.

The recipes come in two formats. The first format is for the experienced brewer who wishes to brew from the ground up, as it were, using malted grains and fresh hops. The second makes use of the enormous variety of can kits now on the market, but adapts them to improve the quality of the finished beer. The recipes have been kept as simple as possible and should be tackled in conjunction with the general information given in Chapter 13 on brewing methods. Specific brands of can kits have not been recommended because the choice is too wide and their availability will vary from place to place.

A glossary is supplied at the end of the book. Here, the reader who encounters any unfamiliar technical terms in the text will be able to obtain a brief explanation.

Finally, the reader should note the following to avoid possible confusion regarding units of measurement used in this book:

- Because brewing in the home is now a worldwide phenomenon, all measurements have been expressed in both metric and US measures. It should be borne in mind that whereas US weights (pounds and ounces) are the same as their old British equivalents, US volume scales differ in that the US pint and gallon are the equivalents of only 0.833 of their Imperial equivalents—or, conversely, one Imperial pint or gallon is the equivalent of 1.2 US pints or gallons.

- Where measurements are expressed in litres, the word has been written in full (rather than using the accepted internation abbreviation 'L'). This has been done to distinguish this parameter from the Lovibond scale for measuring colour (which also uses the abbreviation 'L'). Thus, a volume of five litres is expressed as '5 litres', whereas a colour rating of five on the Lovibond scale is expressed as '5L'.

- In North America, the alcohol level of beer is measured as a proportion of total weight, whereas in the rest of the world it is measured as a proportion of volume. Thus, for every beer for which an alcohol rating is given, it is expressed both ways, with the alc/vol figure first, and the alc/wt figure following in brackets. As alcohol is less dense than water, the alc/wt figure is always lower than the alc/vol figure.

Introduction: It's only beer, isn't it?

Lovers of beer come in two distinct types—those who hold an almost religious attachment to their regular drop and will brook no other, and those who relish beer in whatever shape, size, colour or flavour it may come in.

Loyalty is a sterling quality when it comes to a nation, a marriage or perhaps even a football team, but it is quite misplaced when it comes to beer. If you stick to one standard product, you are likely to be helping no one but some giant brewing conglomerate which is unlikely to repay your loyalty in any tangible way—and you are missing out on a great adventure.

Unfortunately, the single-beer loyalists appear to be in the great majority. And, since the great majority of world beers are bland imitations of the pilsener style, the resulting public image of beer is of a boringly homogeneous product, a pale yellow, fizzy drink that will get you pleasantly tanked after about half a dozen. Beer is beer is beer. It's a commodity. Read about it in the financial pages, and you will discover all sorts of things about market penetration and consumer acceptance but nary a word about the most important things of all. What does it taste like? Is it any good?

Compare this with wine. The writing is all about quality, the bouquet, the flavour, the acid, the tannin, the long finish, the berry notes, the work in the vineyard—all the verbal paraphernalia the wine writers use to try to describe the indescribable. Only occasionally will you read about how well a wine is selling, or whether its makers are in sound financial shape to launch their new joint venture into some as yet untapped market.

And yet beer is at least as interesting and varied as wine. It may well be a more ancient drink; it has, if anything, a wider range of recognisable styles; and far more of it is consumed throughout the world. Even in countries renowned as great wine producers, beer is a popular drink; Spain brews more beer than Holland or Belgium while France produces more than twice as much as Denmark, Sweden or Austria.

Of course, quantity is not quality, but that's only part of the story. In terms of quality, the great beers rank alongside the great wines as treasures of our culture—and they have the advantage of being a lot cheaper. You might have to pay $1000 for a great bottle of vintage burgundy, but a Grande Reserve brewed by the Trappist monks of Chimay in Belgium will cost you about the price of an ordinary bottle of wine, unless you happen to be in Belgium at the time, where it will be a good deal cheaper.

There's a paradox about the price of beer. On the one hand, its very cheapness tells against it. On the other, it is widely expected to be cheap and any beer which dares to ask more for its consumption than the basic price is regarded as too expensive.

Once again the problem is with the mass market, which is widely perceived as being the *only* beer market. The brewing giants claim their beer is the best you can buy because lots of people buy it—and the consumers seem to believe them. But when you stop to think about it, this is nonsense. It's rather like claiming hamburgers and pizzas are the best foods in the world because lots of people buy and eat them. In fact, I once confronted a senior brewery executive with the proposition that his beer was the drinker's equivalent of fast food and he saw nothing to quarrel with in that.

I have nothing against a burger or a takeaway pizza in its proper place—when I'm in a hurry and I simply need to satisfy my hunger—but I wouldn't dream of going out to a leisurely dinner at a fast-food eatery. If I want to savour high-quality food that has been prepared with skill and care, I go to as good a restaurant as I can afford. In the same way, if I've just come off the golf course with a raging thirst I might well throw down a standard world-beer lager; but if I want to savour a quality beer, I will look for something that has been brewed with the intent of making a fine beer, not just to put out a high-selling product at the lowest possible price.

The point is that beer is not just one drink, it's a whole range of drinks of which the dominant, imitation-pilsener style is only one, and by no means the most interesting. Take a good look at the world of beer and you will discover the fruity, living real ales of Britain, the tawny, malty bocks of

Germany, the cleanly pungent dry stouts of Ireland and the kaleidoscopic specialty beers of Belgium. And that's just a small cross-section.

Throughout modern history, four countries or geographical areas have had a crucial influence on the development of beer—Bohemia, Germany, Belgium and the British Isles; and it's no coincidence that today those are the places where you will find most of the great world classic beers.

Not everyone can live in these brewery-blessed places nor can they afford to visit them as often as they might like; and beer exports will never be anything like a viable substitute. Only a small proportion of world beer production is exported, and these beers often deteriorate in transit or while waiting on wholesalers' and retailers' shelves for the fickle demand of an ill-educated market.

And yet, if you have a little patience and are prepared to put in some work and spend only a modest amount of money, you have every chance of drinking almost any of the great beer styles of the world on as regular a basis as you like, wherever you may live. The answer is to brew them yourself.

Home brewing has a very poor public image, an image of strong, pungent brews that will get you drunk in double-quick time and leave you with a stunning hangover next morning. Talk to anyone about it and they will almost invariably regale you with the story of how their dad or uncle or cousin used to brew their own and how the bottles would explode in the middle of the night and wake everyone in fright.

It isn't like that any more. Modern home brewing is a well-regulated, highly skilled craft. In a sense, home brewers have taken the art forward by turning the clock back. They have taken brewing back to the days before it became the business of kings, monasteries or industrialists, to the days when every household brewed its own beer as a matter of course. At the same time they have taken it forward by using the twin advantages of modern technologies and the finest ingredients.

It is now possible to brew in your own home a beer as good as almost anything you can buy and better than most which are on offer. And, by brewing in essentially the same way as the commercial brewers (but on a minuscule scale) and using the same ingredients, you can replicate nearly any style of beer. With the variety of ingredients and equipment on today's home-brewing market, the world is your oyster. As I write, in my home just outside Sydney, Australia, I am lagering a Munich-style helles lager in a fridge especially adapted for the purpose, while a keg of Irish red ale sits in my cellar waiting to be tapped. Another fridge contains two kegs both attached to serving taps—one of pale ale, the other of Scottish heavy.

That's not to say that you can expect to brew a beer which is an exact copy of a commercial product you might admire and wish to replicate, say a Fuller's London Pride or a Warsteiner Pils. It is extremely difficult to copy a particular beer style, even with the most advanced and expensive

equipment. For example, Carlsberg brewed in Copenhagen, Denmark, is quite different from what is supposedly the same beer brewed in Northampton, England. Matilda Bay in Western Australia brews a version of the famous Belgian lager Stella Artois; it's a fine beer, but considerably different from the original. If the big brewers can't do it, home brewers, with their limited equipment and resources, have even less chance. However, because the home brewer is not brewing to a budget, as any commercial operation is, he or she can brew a beer in the general style of a country or area which will probably be different in all sorts of subtle ways, but not necessarily inferior to the original.

Even if you are not prepared to brew like the big boys from the original malted grains—and it does take time and some hard work—the choice of easy can kits is so extensive now that, in 20 minutes, you can put together a brew that will give you some sort of approximation of the real thing and will almost certainly prove interesting and flavoursome enough to make a welcome change from the standard big-brewery offerings.

The final advantage is that home brewing saves you so much money, particularly when you brew from the original grains. Even costing in the price of equipment, electricity and water (but not labour!), a 330 ml (US 12 fl oz) bottle of high-quality beer brewed this way costs me no more than 20 cents, and usually much less. That compares ridiculously well with the price of commercial beer anywhere in the world.

The home-brewing movement just seems to grow and grow, both in sheer size and in quality. It has spread its benign tentacles all over the world and it keeps in touch with its outflung units through clubs, books, magazines and now the Internet. It is the repository of a vast amount of information about beer and the ingredients and techniques that are used to make it. If you really want to know about beer, ask a home brewer. Better still, become a home brewer.

An interesting shift is taking place in the world of beer. On the one hand, the world's big-selling beers seem to become ever more bland, as the big brewers shift from using whole hops of any sort, let alone fine aroma hops, and the search for the fragrance of Saaz or Hallertauer hops in a standard beer becomes a less and less rewarding pastime. In Germany recently, on a research trip for this book, I ordered a kristall wheat beer at Frankfurt airport. It was brought to me with a slice of lemon in it. Of course, I sent it back and they took out the lemon but such flavour as the beer may have had (it was not one of the great classics of the style) had been destroyed. And this was in Germany, which prides itself on being *the* beer country—never mind what the Belgians may say.

On the one hand, everywhere in the world, the salesmen of blandness and gimmickry are creeping in, turning mass-produced beer into no more than a commodity, 'Fosterising the world', as one executive once described it; on the other, home brewers and micro-brewers have started a new surge of interest in beer as a work of craft if not art. In the United States, home of some of the world's blandest beers, the number of breweries has risen from 90 to more than 800 in the past 20 years. And they are not brewing Budweiser! Beer tourism is on the upsurge, particularly in California where it's now possible to take tours of the breweries, tasting as you go, rather as you would go around the vineyards, sampling their individual products.

Even if you don't have the desire or the time to brew your own specialties, don't give up on good beer. It's all around you waiting to be discovered. Start looking now.

What is beer?

The *Concise Oxford Dictionary* defines beer as 'alcoholic liquor (esp. of lighter kinds) from fermented malt, etc., flavoured with hops, etc.' Microsoft's *Encarta* describes a standard American beer as containing on average '90 per cent water, 3.5 per cent alcohol by weight, 0.5 per cent carbon dioxide and 6 per cent extractives consisting of proteins, carbohydrates, minerals and aromatic flavourings'.

That tells you what goes into beer and what comes out but it doesn't tell you the important part: the process, how the ingredients and flavourings are transformed by the magic of yeast into the most beautiful drink yet devised by humankind.

The key ingredient in beer is yeast; you can make beer without barley and beer without hops but you can't make beer without yeast. It is the action of the yeast turning sugars into alcohol and carbon dioxide that creates beer.

The primary source of these fermentable sugars is malted barley, although many beers use a proportion of sugars from other sources—mainly corn sugar and rice in the United States, wheat in some German and Belgian beers, and cane sugar in Britain and Australia.

All grains contain a large proportion of starch; brewing involves changing these starches into sugars then further converting these sugars, or most of them, into alcohol and carbon dioxide gas, giving the beer its alcoholic kick and its fizz.

But the process begins before the grain gets near the brewery; first the grain has to be modified so that these starches can be worked on in the brewing process.

This step is called malting and it involves soaking the grain in water until it germinates, that is, sends up a tiny shoot. By one of those happy coincidences that makes the brewing of beer possible, while this is happening, the starches in the grain undergo changes that make them ready to be converted into sugars. As soon as the grain has sprouted to the desired extent, it is heated in kilns to dry it, stop further activity and remove the tiny shoots. It is now malted grain, or simply malt. This malt is the brewer's principal raw material; it is the basis from which more than 99 per cent of the world's beers are made, whether they be pale lagers or the darkest of stouts.

In the brewing process itself, the first task is to convert the starch in the malted barley into fermentable sugars. This is done by a process known as mashing—a word probably derived from ancient practices, which predate the use of malt, in which bread was mashed into warm water to extract the sugars. In the modern system, used for the past several centuries, the malt is covered in hot water and left to steep at carefully predetermined temperatures for an hour or more. (These temperatures and times vary according to the style of beer to be made.)

At the end of the predetermined time all or most of the sugar in the malt should have been dissolved into the water. The resulting sugary liquid, known as sweet wort (pronounced *wert*), is then drained off and, at the same time, more hot water is rinsed through the grains to flush out all available sugar into the wort. This process is known as 'sparging'.

Now the wort is boiled with a measured amount of hops. These are a kind of pale green flower which, when boiled with a malt solution, give out a strong bitterness and a distinctive flavour and aroma. The boiling also helps to clear the wort by precipitating out materials such as proteins, which would otherwise stay in suspension in the beer and later give it an unpleasantly cloudy appearance.

Next the wort has to be cooled from boiling point down to the temperature at which it is possible to add (or pitch) the yeast. The yeast is a living organism and is no better than we are at surviving huge extremes of temperature. Yeast can survive temperatures up to nearly 50°C (122°F), but its optimum working temperatures are much lower than that. As we will see later, there are two basic kinds of beer-brewing yeasts—ale yeasts, which work best in the range of 15 to 22°C (60–72°F), and lager yeasts, which are most comfortable between 8 and 14°C (48–57°F).

Once the yeast is pitched into the wort, it goes to work, multiplying rapidly, then consuming the fermentable sugars. In its place, the yeast leaves two highly useful waste products, alcohol and carbon dioxide. Most of the carbon dioxide from this primary fermentation is simply dissipated into the air but, of course, the alcohol remains as an integral part of the finished beer.

In naturally conditioned beers, some of this carbon dioxide may be retained by transferring the beer to a sealed container such as a bottle or keg. The CO_2 produced then dissolves into the beer and is released when the bottle is opened or beer is drawn from the keg. This gives the beer its familiar sparkle and fizz. However, in most cases the carbonation is added artificially, simply by pumping in CO_2 under pressure until it dissolves into the beer.

The effect is much the same; in the end, you have in front of you a glass or bottle of beer. Enjoy it!

2 The history of beer

Beer in the ancient world

In the beginning there was ... beer. Beer is one of the oldest known creations of humankind. It is older than civilisation, older than cities, older than nations. Humans may have started brewing it as early as 10 000 BC, and it was certainly a part of our earliest recorded history.

The first civilisation which has left us any written records of beer brewing is that of Sumer, a kingdom that grew up as an amalgamation of a number of settlements in the Fertile Crescent, the Tigris–Euphrates basin, in the Middle East around 3000 BC. The Sumerians developed agriculture based on a system of irrigation and it was this on which their prosperity and their cities were founded. The best known of these cities was Ur, the first capital of Sumer and a name that was to recur in a very significant way in the history of beer.

The Sumerians also developed crafts and industries—and the cuneiform script, a system of symbols that was to dominate written communications in the area for 2000 years. In this script they left a number of useful and fascinating records, including the narrative poem 'The Epic of Gilgamesh', a romanticised story of one of their kings, Gilgamesh, who ruled the city of Uruk or Erechs.

According to the epic, the gods created Enkidu, a wild, bestial man who apparently ate grass, and sent him to challenge Gilgamesh to a wrestling match. To be on the safe side, before the contest, Gilgamesh sent a courtesan to Enkidu to test his strengths and weaknesses. In the time Enkidu spent with her she taught him some of the niceties of civilisation.

'Enkidu knew not what bread was nor how one ate it,' the epic relates. 'He had also not learned to drink beer. The woman opened her mouth and spoke to Enkidu: "Eat the bread now, O Enkidu, as it belongs to life. Drink also beer, as it is the custom of the land." Enkidu drank seven cups of beer and his heart soared. In this condition, he washed himself and became a human being.'

Gilgamesh and Enkidu went on to become close friends—some say the biblical story of David and Jonathan was based on their friendship—but that's not our concern here. The passage from the epic tells us a couple of important things about the place of beer in Sumerian society. Clearly beer drinking was not considered, as it often is today, as some kind of vice but rather as almost a sacred duty, something that separated man from beast. More mundanely, it indicates that beer was drunk from cups, at least in the time when the epic was written in about 2000 BC, which raises the possibility that some of the earliest pottery vessels manufactured by man were made in order to drink beer.

Some have even gone so far as to suggest that beer was one of the major factors in the development of civilisation. The thinking is that if beer had been developed to this level of sophistication by the Sumerians, it is not unreasonable to assume that it must have existed in some form in more primitive societies. Its value to society would have been its promotion of good health. Until very recent times, water supplies have been at best a risky proposition for drinking. Even before the establishment of settlements, it must have been commonplace for waterholes to become accidentally poisoned by the corpses of animals; and whenever people have gathered in settlements, one of the results has been that they have made the water unfit or dangerous to drink until the creation of the kind of high-quality water reticulation systems we have in developed countries today. Beer, having been boiled and fermented and thus containing a reasonable percentage of alcohol, was safe from further infection and would therefore keep for a couple of weeks or so and be safe to drink. In many cases it might have been the basic drinking supply for all kinds of activities, from working in the fields to building houses and even going to war. This, as we will see, has been one of beer's major roles throughout the ages.

Its health-giving properties would also have been an incentive to grow more barley and meant an extension of cultivation, which would in turn have led to the expansion of fixed settlements and ultimately to the establishment of cities. It may be drawing a long bow–but beer just might be one of the main reasons for the establishment of civilisation itself.

The Sumerians have also left us the first accounts of how beer was made, which give a graphic meaning to the word 'mash', the term used by modern-day brewers to describe the process of extracting sugars from grain in order to turn them into an alcoholic drink.

It appears that beer developed as an accidental by-product of bread making. Since the existence of yeast was unknown, the first bread must have been fermented by accident, by wild yeasts, which got into the dough and made it rise. As still happens with sourdough bread, some of this successful dough would have been kept aside and used to start new fermentations and thus a constant supply of fermentable material would have been to hand.

At some stage, someone must have mixed this bread, or possibly even the unbaked bread dough, again presumably by accident, with water at the right temperature for enzymes in the grain to go to work and convert the starches in the grain to sugar which would then have been leached out into the water. This primitive wort (the word breweries use to describe unfermented beer), if left alone for a few days, would have started fermenting, either because of the yeast culture in the bread or through the action of wild yeasts in the air or in the surrounding woodwork and buildings.

You would think the resulting brew must have been fairly horrible to look at and none too wonderful on the nose, but perhaps these early 'brewers' were lucky and a particularly friendly yeast had got into it so that the aroma and flavour were interesting and enticing rather than repellent, or perhaps it took years or even centuries of trial and error to get it right. In any case, someone must have been tempted to drink the brew and become the first human to feel the effects of alcohol. It's a moment in human history that is seldom considered–but just imagine being the first ever human to feel the euphoria of intoxication!

So, the Sumerians developed a system of soaking a mash of bread, whether fully baked, half-baked or otherwise, in water, then left the yeasts to do the work of fermenting it in a kind of combination of mash tun and fermenting vessel. In fact this container was probably the vessel in which the brew was served as well—and it may well have been used over and over again, thus establishing a strain of almost domesticated yeasts, although hardly a pure or sophisticated strain!

To drink this thick porridgy beer, it is believed they used straws in order to avoid picking up the remnants of dough, although 'The Epic of Gilgamesh' seems to indicate that at some stage they had got around to straining the liquid off the solids and were able to use cups.

The Sumerians used a mixture of wheat and barley to make these beers but it is not known whether the bread they used was baked specifically for beer making or whether beer making was just a way of using stale or leftover loaves. The brewers were women, the ordinary housewives of the time to whom making beer was just another part of household work, like cooking. This domination of brewing by women was to continue until relatively modern times when it became a money-making trade and was then taken over by men.

The Sumerian empire was overrun in about 2000 BC by the Babylonians who continued the art of brewing and helped spread it through the Middle East. The Babylonians brought further sophistication to the art and went as far as to classify 20 different kinds of beer they could produce, including one that was stored for a period to stabilise it for export to Egypt, a primitive precursor of the beer style that was eventually to conquer most of the world—lager.

The laws of the Babylonian King Hammurabi, the first known legal code, included one establishing a daily beer ration, which was measured according to the social status of the individual. Ordinary people were allowed 2 litres a day, government workers 3 litres and priests 5 litres, perhaps the first sign of the legends that were to grow up all over the world about rapacious civil servants, jolly friars and cheerful monks. The code also laid down punishments for

making inferior beer, the worst of which was being drowned in your own brew. It is this kind of evidence of the legal standing of beer which indicates its vital importance in the ancient world.

The Egyptians were quick to take up brewing and eventually used beer, which they called *kash*, as a form of currency to facilitate trade—the first cash economy. Much later, around 60 BC, their Queen Cleopatra, famous for having flings with Julius Caesar and his protégé Mark Anthony, even introduced the first known beer tax.

By this time, beer had begun to go into a decline in the Mediterranean area with the rise to power first of the Greeks and then the Romans. Because they occupied land, which was particularly suited to the growing of grapes, both of these cultures venerated wine as the drink of the Gods and tended to despise beer as an inferior drink. In the Middle East, the rise of Islam and its code of abstinence spelled the death knell for Egyptian brewing and, in the early centuries of the millennium, beer, while it never vanished from the civilised world, lost its status and importance. It was to return with a vengeance, however.

As the Roman Empire, having taken in most of the territory surrounding the Mediterranean, expanded northwards around the start of the first millennium, it ran into a quite different culture, that of the wild tribes of the central European heartland.

Brewing had become established among these tribes hundreds of years earlier. The first archaeological evidence dates from a site near Kulmbach in Germany where beer containers dating from around 800 BC have been found. Interestingly, Kulmbach is still a major brewing centre. Other evidence is to be found in the Nordic sagas, the *Edda* and the *Kalevala*, which both devote considerable space to beer. In fact the *Kalevala*, the Finnish national epic, gives twice as much space to beer as it does to the creation of the world itself. It seems the early Finns had a fine sense of proportion.

When the Roman legions advanced into the forest of Germany they encountered Teutonic tribes such as the Visigoths, the Huns, the Vandals, the Franks and Burgundians, all beer-drinking cultures. Naturally they despised them and their coarse drink.

'To drink, the Teutons have a horrible brew fermented from barley or wheat, a brew which has only a far removed similarity to wine,' the historian Cornelius Tacitus wrote in *Germania*, his celebrated study of the Germans.

In the long run, the beer drinkers were to have the last laugh. Even though the Romans conquered Gaul, and even most of Britain, they never quite managed to subdue Germany and eventually the barbarians poured south to capture and sack Rome itself. Thus the Western world was plunged into what Westerners know as the Dark Ages, a time which was to see beer arise like a slow fermentation and become the dominant drink of northern Europe and a beverage to rival the best of the fruits of the vine.

Beer in the Middle Ages

In the turmoil that followed the collapse of Rome, social structures fell apart, but out in the countryside where the great majority of people lived, life went on more or less as normal. Making beer was part of this normality and was the job of the women of the house, in much the same way as cooking and minding the children. In this way brewing was kept alive until once more organised cities and states began to coalesce out of the chaos. As they did, they sought to take control over this vital element in society.

FIGURE 2.1
From earliest times, monks were active in growing hops and brewing beer. During Lent, beer replaced food to a large extent. In Bavaria, the expression 'liquid bread' is still used.
THE HOP ATLAS 1994, P.25, JOH. BARTH & SOHN, NUREMBERG

The regime that took over in Europe was the feudal system, a strict top-to-bottom hierarchy, which ruled the lives of all. At the top was the king, beneath him the nobles, beneath them their vassal landholders, and beneath them the common people or serfs. Each tier paid tribute in the form of labour or produce to the tier above and in turn received protection from those above, in theory at least. God was in his heaven and all was well with the world. However, speaking of God, a new element entered this mix around the eighth century, an element that was to play an important part in the history and development of brewing, and in some place still does—the monasteries.

Christianity had been introduced to Italy in the time of the Romans but the first northern Europeans to be converted were the Irish, followed by the Scots and the English. From there, evangelistic monks spread the faith steadily through Europe. As they went, they established monasteries as spiritual strongholds. These became quite substantial communities and it was a natural process that they should brew their own beer simply to establish a safe drinking supply. Monasteries were also places where travellers on the inhospitable roads of the time could find shelter and sustenance, and beer would have been part of that sustenance. Another spur to beer consumption in the monasteries was that beer did not count as food in times of fasting.

Some of the monasteries went a good deal further than that, however. The monastery at St Gall, in what is now Switzerland, founded by a disciple of the Irish St Columba as early as 590 as a simple, spartan community, by 800 had developed into a very sophisticated community—and one of the biggest breweries in the world at the time. It seems to have been here that the division of beer into three qualities took place. The highest quality, and strongest, was reserved for the abbot and his guests; the second was a normal beer called *cervisa* for the everyday consumption of the monks; the third was a thinner version, a kin of 'small beer', brewed for the abbey's secular employees and for charity. Interestingly enough this division is still celebrated today in the Trappist breweries of Belgium, which often brew three styles of increasing strength: single, double and triple.

About the same time the Benedictine monk Corbinian founded a small chapel on the hill of Weihenstephan, near present-day Munich. By 1040 it had risen to the status of an abbey and was granted the right to sell its beer. The brewery is still there today and claims to be the world's oldest continuously operating brewery; it also has close links with the brewing university and research centre of the same name.

The beer of this time did not use hops, except perhaps incidentally, as a major ingredient. Instead it was flavoured with a combination of herbs which varied considerably from place to place and from brewer to brewer. Some of the herbs commonly used included aromatics and bitterers like sweet gale, juniper, yarrow, pine resin and sage. The mix was called 'gruit', and because the herbs grew on open land that belonged to the crown, the right to harvest and sell it became strictly controlled, giving the rulers of the various states their first real control over beer production.

Hops had been known and cultivated since the eighth century but it took another 200 or more years before they became generally accepted as the main flavouring of beer. The great Abbess Hildegard of Bingen, a remarkable woman who, among other things, wrote music and had visions which today seem remarkably similar to tales of close encounters with people from flying saucers, was one of the early propagandists for hops in her treatise *Physica Sacra* (*Sacred World*), in which she commented on the flavouring and preserving qualities of hops in beer. She lived to be 81 so perhaps she had something there.

The use of hops originated in what is now the Czech Republic and spread west and north over the next 300 years, reaching Holland in around 1300. From there the Dutch exported them to Britain and by 1500 the use of herbs in beer had virtually died out except for special uses, although it has been revived recently by small specialist breweries, mainly in Belgium.

The other major development in the Middle Ages was the steady rise of secular, commercial breweries to compete with and largely supersede the monasteries. By the end of the twelfth century there were more than 500 monastery breweries in Germany alone and similar numbers elsewhere, but this was the high point of monastery brewing. The success of the monasteries made it obvious to the secular authorities that brewing was a potentially lucrative business so the feudal lords began to establish their own court brewhouses or *Hofbräuhausen*. Next, the wealthy burghers of the burgeoning cities, particularly in the more secular northern Europe, started to move into the business. Brewing became a secular craft, guilds were formed and a whole array of new legislation was created to try to regulate the trade. There were protectionist laws keeping out 'foreign' beers—which meant simply the beers brewed in other cities; there were laws about the sizes and shapes of beer measures and there were laws about what should and should not be put into beer.

Only one of these laws has stood the test of time and is still adhered to by German brewers of the present day. In 1447 the city of Munich made a law proscribing the use of anything but barley malt, hops and water to make beer (they didn't know of the existence of yeast at the time). Then in 1516, the rulers of Bavaria, Dukes Wilhelm IV and Ludwig X, introduced the famous purity law, the *Reinheitsgebot*, essentially adopting the law of Munich that only barley, hops and water could be used to brew a beer. This law was eventually adopted all across Germany (but nowhere else in the world) in 1906 and remained in legal force until the sad day in 1987 when the European Court ruled it was not compatible with the free trade policy of the European Community and struck it out. It is all the more to the credit of German brewers that, although the law no longer has any force, they have stood by it completely and still do not brew with anything but malt (barley or wheat), hops, water and, of course, yeast.

Beer in the modern era

Although brewing had become commercialised, it was still done on a small scale by modern standards and most breweries were what are still called in Germany house-breweries, which meant that the brewery was part of a public house or tavern of some sort. Over the next two centuries however, the economics of production pushed more and more brewers to specialise simply in brewing and forget about running pubs, while publicans found it easier and cheaper to buy beer in bulk from commercial or 'common' brewers. The British beer industry was to the forefront of this change and it was a development in England that led to the next major step in brewing, the rise of the mass-market commercial brewery.

Britain was the frontrunner of the Industrial Revolution. In the mid eighteenth century, as new machinery made large-scale production possible, particularly in the textile industries, and the enclosure of rural lands left huge numbers of rural families penniless, they poured into the cities in search of jobs in the 'dark Satanic mills' and factories. These newly created industrial workers, working long, hard hours, created a huge potential market. By a happy coincidence there was beer ready to step in and fill the needs of that market.

Tradition has it that porter was invented by a brewer named Ralph Harwood in London in 1722. Beer was then served in three styles, presumably in varying degrees of strength, much in the way the monks of St Gall produced their three grades of beer. However, so many customers, so the story goes, were in the habit of ordering a mix of the three styles, known as Three Threads, that Harwood decided to brew a beer that combined the qualities of all three. He called this brew Entire, or Entire Butt. However, beer writer and historian Terry Foster disputes this story as being too simple and unlikely. Instead he suggests that porter was a result simply of improved brewing technique. Nowadays when beer is made, the next step after the mash is sparging or rinsing the grains with extra water to extract as much as possible of the fermentable sugars from them, but in the early eighteenth century brewers had not yet worked out this technique. Instead they would mash the grains and drain off the first, and strongest, wort; then they would add hot water and mash the same grains again, drawing off a second, lighter wort; finally they would mash and drain off a third time.

The resulting beers were generally known as strong beer, common beer and small beer. What the porter brewers did was to combine the three worts into one beer. The total amount of wort produced from the process was known as the 'gyle', so the beer became known as Entire Gyle or simply Entire. Because the technique required more expensive equipment, more space and more time, particularly to age the beer, it was beyond the means of small brewers and thus was ideally suited for bigger operations. Its huge popularity gave its makers the impetus needed to establish themselves on a much bigger scale than had been economical before this point.

The name 'porter' arrived later, either because it was the drink of the London porters or because when the beer was delivered to a public house the delivery man would call out 'Porter!' The appeal of this second explanation for the name is that it emphasises the change that had come over the beer trade—that wholesale brewing was now the norm. The porter boom helped set up some of the major breweries of London (the modern giant Whitbread's is an example), and showed others that growth was the way ahead. From being only a London beer, porter spread out all over England and then eventually across the Irish Sea to Dublin where the Guinness brewery, established in 1759, took it up with great and ongoing success. Porter retained its domination of the British market for another hundred years before it was challenged by a new usurper, pale ale.

Pale ale, which had been around since at least the early years of the eighteenth century, wasn't actually particularly pale except by comparison with the chocolatey-dark porter; the colour was, and is, amber to brown. At first it was relatively expensive compared with porter because the lighter malts were more costly for the maltsters to produce. With improved techniques of malting and brewing, the price of pale ales began to fall steadily, and the increased use of industrially produced glass for drinking vessels in the 1840s spurred on the demand for paler, clearer beers. By the 1850s, the city of Burton-on-Trent, partly thanks to its suitable water supply, had become the major pale ale centre, exporting its beer all over the country as communications by road, canal and finally railway, improved rapidly. Speaking of exports, it was a very particular export market that helped create the most famous of pale ales, India Pale Ale (IPA). The nineteenth century was Britain's imperial heyday and its troops were scattered all over the globe, literally holding the fort for the Empire. The greatest concentration of them was in that jewel in the imperial crown, India. In those days, even more than now, troops needed beer–water supplies were even worse in India than they were in Britain (and they were not too good there, as repeated outbreaks of cholera in London testified). To transport beer to India took weeks in sailing ships and involved passing through a wide range of temperatures, from freezing to extremely hot and humid. To preserve the beer on this risky journey it was brewed to a higher alcoholic strength than the standard pale ale and was given a heavier dose of hops. Drinkers at home got to know of this big, full-flavoured beer and demanded it be sold in Britain as well. Brewers, of course, were only too happy to oblige and IPA became a permanent part of the standard British beer repertoire, as it still is.

Meanwhile in Europe significant developments were taking place. The most important of them was the discovery of a new technique of fermentation that was to revolutionise the world of brewing. Until the early

FIGURE 2.2

Beer has always been important to troops— German soldiers in 1915

BEHRINGER, *LÖWENBRÄU*, MUNICH 1991, P. 225

years of the nineteenth century, all fermentations were conducted at ambient temperatures with yeasts that tended to rise to the surface of the beer. This was handy because the yeast could be skimmed off the top and used to start new fermentations. However, in the summer months, particularly in the southern regions of Germany, this kind of brewing was always a risky business as the heat and the prevalence of wild yeasts and bacteria in the air could make fermentation turn sour. So, as early as 1553, the State of Bavaria banned brewing in the summer months. The brewers now had to brew enough beer over the winter to last them through the summer; what's more, they had to find some place to store the beer.

Bavaria is close to the Alps and is dotted with sandstone hills. It was on those hills that powerful nobles of the state and the church built their fortresses. On and around these hills, towns and eventually cities grew up as folk of lesser position sought the safety of powerful protectors.

Naturally, brewers were among the craftsmen and tradesmen who congregated in the towns. They got their water supplies from wells cut into the porous sandstone and cut cellars in the same soft but firm rock. These cellars maintained (and still maintain) a relatively constant temperature, ranging only from around 4 to 10°C (40 to 50°F) throughout the year, so they proved the ideal place to store beer. Over years of storing their beer at these quite low temperatures, the Bavarian brewers noticed that their yeasts began to change their behaviour. Over the long storage period the top-fermenting yeasts died off but other strains, which could still live and work at these lower temperatures, took their place. So fermentation went on very slowly during this storage period, creating carbonation in the beer and helping preserve it during the long wait for the following winter. These yeasts flocculated (gathered into large clumps) and dropped to the bottom of the beer, allowing the brewers to decant the clear beer off the yeast for

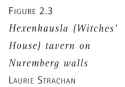

FIGURE 2.3
Hexenhausla (Witches' House) tavern on Nuremberg walls
LAURIE STRACHAN

distribution in kegs and barrels. Eventually it became standard practice to conduct all the fermentation at temperatures of around 10°C (50°F)—and so the technique of bottom-fermentation was discovered. The German word for 'to store' or 'to put away' is *lagern*, so beers made by bottom-fermentation and long storage became known as lagers. Top-fermented beers, on the other hand, are usually classified as ales.

Unfortunately the technique could not be used without the necessary stability of temperature, and not every brewing community was in the fortunate position of the Bavarians in having huge areas of natural cold storage. So the technique remained a Bavarian, or at least southern, European specialty until the late nineteenth century, when another major technical innovation made it possible for anyone, anywhere, to do it. That innovation was the invention of refrigeration—but first came another development in Bohemia, just across the border from Bavaria, which was to change to appearance of beer forever.

Bohemia—now the Czech Republic—has always been an important brewing centre. The oldest written references to brewing in Bohemia date back to 768. The Bohemians were also leaders in the growing of hops and their use in beer. Until the late eighteenth century, the Czechs had a system of licensing private houses to brew beer on a number of occasions each year; this beer would then be distributed to the other households until it was their turn to brew. In the city of Plzen (Pilsen) this clumsy system was abandoned in 1786 and permanent public houses were established. However, they also proved far from perfect and by 1838 the quality of the beer being produced was considered just too low to tolerate. The last straw appears to have been a batch that was so bad that 36 casks of it were tipped out into the gutters. So, the city council decided to finance an official city brewery, to be called the Burghers' Brewery. To this end they commissioned an architect called Stelzr and sent him on a fact-finding tour to Germany. Stelzr came back not only with plans for the most modern brewery that could be built but with a Bavarian master brewer, Josef Groll.

Groll was highly experienced in Bavarian bottom-fermenting techniques and now he was given the task of using these skills to produce a high-quality beer using only local Czech ingredients. Fortunately these were (and still are) as good as any available anywhere. The superb pilsener malt is still considered the basic standard for lager malts, and Zatec or Saaz hops are acknowledged to be among the finest aroma hops in the world. Set the task of creating a new beer, Groll experimented with using only pale malts, which had just become available in Bohemia, and came up with the single most important beer that has even been brewed. It was pale, though probably not as pale as modern lagers, and it was highly hopped with the low-bitterness Saaz hops. And it was a runaway success. At a time when the Bohemian crystal industry was booming it looked brilliant in clear drinking vessels and it must have tasted like nectar to those used to the dark, cloudy beers that were the norm at the time.

The Pilsen brewery was soon selling it to the Germans and it was the brewery's agent in Berlin who gave it the name it has kept till the present day–Pilsner Urquell. Naturally German brewers began to copy the successful style, which became generically known as pilsner or pilsener, and from there it swept the beer-drinking world. Nowadays the vast majority of the beer consumed in the world is based on that pilsener style, although individual brewers and different countries have given it their own twist. The Germans, although sticking to the original all-malt formulation, have developed a paler, lighter style than the original Czech brew, while the Dutch and Scandinavians have taken lightness even further and exported their version of it all over the world. The problem now is that some of the beers produced under the name pilsener bear no more than a token resemblance to the original, as drinkers in the United States and Australia can testify.

The great pilsener conquest left a few enclaves. Small areas of Germany still cling to the old top-fermenting techniques. In Cologne and Düsseldorf, top-fermented beers are the standard while beers made from a proportion of malted wheat as well as barley, a traditional Bavarian style, are growing rapidly in popularity all over Germany.

However, the most notable centres of ale brewing and drinking are the British Isles and Belgium. In Britain and Ireland, ales were still the most popular drink until well after World War II, but in the 1960s and '70s a new wave of draught lager threatened to wash over the traditional bitters, milds and stouts. The invasion was given a helping hand by British brewers themselves, who began to abandon their traditional methods of packaging beer and adopted lager-style packaging.

To understand the difference this made you first have to grasp one fundamental fact about traditional British beer–it is a fresh product, not an aged one. British bitters and milds are not lagered or otherwise stored to mature, they are sold while the beer is still young and the yeast is still active. This is tied in with the fact that to this day, the great majority of beer consumed in Britain is out of the tap, not from bottles or cans. Around this a whole skill of cellaring developed as the cellarmen learned how to handle the living beer. Most importantly they had to know exactly when the beer was ready to start serving and thus how long they should leave it in the cellar before tapping it. By contrast, lagers are, by definition, lagered or stored to mature and stabilise. They are usually filtered and often pasteurised. So, when they reach the pub they can be simply left to sit and tapped when the demand arises. Apart from prolonged storage after pasteurisation, when they are at risk of oxidisation, they are unlikely to come to any harm. Naturally this ease of handling greatly appealed to publicans so British brewers started filtering and even pasteurising their milds and bitters and packaging them in pressurised kegs. The problem with storing beer under high CO_2 pressure is that the gas dissolves into the beer, completely altering its character. From a smooth, slightly spritzig but still fairly flat drink, it becomes fizzy and prickly on the tongue and the kinds of subtle flavours associated with a living beer are largely lost—the beer becomes a kind of ersatz dark lager.

Fortunately, the brewers ran into some opposition. A group of journalists and others got together to fight what they saw as a major threat to real British beer. They called themselves the Campaign for Real Ale. CAMRA has been described as the world's most successful consumer organisation and there must be some truth to that, for its campaigns slowed, then virtually halted, the destruction of the traditional British beer. What's more, its dissemination of information has resulted in a new level of education about beer among the British public. As a regular visitor to Britain, it has been wonderful to see each time I return, a growing number of pubs where you can find Real Ale, traditional-style British beer served from unpressurised casks, and the establishment and revival of small breweries dedicated to brewing one of the great drinks of the world, something which is an integral part of British culture. However, the battle is never over; lagers still account for around 50 per cent of British beer consumption and it is a sobering thought (literally) to realise that, at the last count, the single biggest-selling beer in the country was a feeble British copy of what is already in its native Australia a fairly ordinary beer—Foster's Lager.

In Belgium, lagers took an even firmer hold and they now account for around 75 per cent of consumption. However, at the same time as CAMRA started its battle in Britain, the Belgians in their own individualistic way started to fight back.

Belgium was fortunate in that it had retained some aspects and styles of brewing that had completely vanished in virtually every other nation. And, just as the tide of conformity and mass production looked like consigning some of these techniques to history, the Belgians, in a kind of reaction against the pressure, started to revive them. The revival started in the 1950s but really took off in the 1960s as brewers and

FIGURE 2.4
Traditional English ale pub
FULLER SMITH & TURNER PLC

drinkers, perhaps rebelling against the uniformity of the north European pilsener, rediscovered the delights of Belgian specialty ales. In a sense this was history repeating itself, for once again it was monasteries that led the way. The five Trappist monasteries of Belgium had always been centres of brewing and after the war they began to sell their beer on the open market, spurring interest in traditional brewing throughout Belgium.

Trappist beers vary greatly from cloister to cloister but they have one thing in common— they are a far cry from pilsener. Some are dark and malty, some are pale and hoppy, some are amber and smooth; nearly all have some sort of unusual yeast character that would be characterised by a conventional brewer as an infection; most are very strong by normal standards; few show very much in the way of bitterness; all are top-fermented. The classic Trappist classification, as exemplified by the beers of Westmalle, is into three grades—single, double and triple. The single, a beer of conventional strength, has not traditionally been sold to the public but the double and triple have. Westmalle's double (dubbel) is a dark, malty beer of around 6–7% alc/vol (5–6% alc/wt), while the triple (trippel) is pale gold, richly flavoured and highly aromatic. Secular brewers have adopted the classifications, but other Trappists sometimes do it differently. Chimay, the biggest of the five monastery brewers, also divides its beer into three styles, but they are all brown beers and the differences in strength are not nearly as pronounced; while Orval produces one product, a golden-amber ale of around conventional strength but far from ordinary flavour.

Trappist beers have spawned many imitations and have been the catalyst for a wave of revivals of old, strong ale styles in Belgium. In parallel with that, other old styles have been revived—most notably white beer, made from barley malt and unmalted wheat. And all the time, the oldest form of brewing, a form that dates all the way back to the beginning has never died out.

Belgium was and is the only place where brewing by spontaneous fermentation—brewing without adding yeast, a process analogous to sourdough bread making—never died out. In the Payottenland west of Brussels, traditional brewers still make beer this way, just by opening the windows and letting the wild yeasts and bacteria in. The resulting beer is known as a lambic beer and the principal drinking style, created by blending old and new batches, is called gueuze. Even stranger beers are made by adding fruit to the lambic and fermenting it once more. These are styles that have to be experienced to be believed but they show just how wide and varied the world of beer can be.

Belgium these days is a hotbed of experimentation as the past meets the present and heads for the future, but perhaps the most amazing beer revival in recent years has taken place in the United States.

Even before the arrival of Europeans, a kind of beer-brewing was carried out by the native Americans, using corn instead of barley, but beer, more or less as we know it now, arrived with the colonists. It appears that the Pilgrim Fathers made their historic landing at Plymouth Rock in Massachusetts not by plan but because their beer supplies—so necessary in a time when water was not safe to drink—were running out. They must have carried a lot of beer in the *Mayflower* because each of the colonists was allotted a ration of two quarts a day. It doesn't sound too puritanical by today's standards. As settlement spread, so did brewing, and some of the notables of early American history were known to have been brewers—George Washington brewed his own beer (the recipe still exists) as well as importing English porter, William Penn had a brewery, and Thomas Jefferson, Patrick Henry, James Madison and, notably, Samuel Adams, were strong advocates of a local brewing industry.

Naturally the beer brewed in those days was modelled on the British top-fermented ale but in the mid-nineteenth century all this changed. A new wave of immigrants from Germany arrived and with them they brought bottom-fermenting technology. Soon afterwards the invention of refrigeration made lager brewing possible in any climate and at any time of year. Many of the famous names in US beer, Anheuser, Stroh, Coors, Schlitz, Pabst and Weinhard among them, established themselves in this period. The beers they brewed were based on German models, but they had a problem: the malt generally available in America at the time was made from 6-row barley, which did not give the same characteristics as European 2-row varieties. The brewers found their beer was too heavy when brewed with only malt, so they started using a portion of a readily available cereal, corn, in its place to lighten the body and the colour. The drinkers took to the new formulation and this was the genesis of the style now known as American light.

By the 1870s there were more than 4000 breweries in the United States but this was a peak that was never reached again. Refrigeration and more stable beers allowed big brewers to transport their beers to distant markets and their economies of scale allowed them to out-compete smaller rivals, so the process of consolidation, common to every beer market, began to take on speed. Then came World War I and a wave of anti-German sentiment. Brewers became easy targets for the new forces of temperance, which were rising in the Midwest and spreading their tentacles across the country. In 1920 the Volstead Act was passed, banning the sale or consumption of alcoholic beverages throughout the United States. The 13 years of Prohibition decimated American brewing and it never recovered its diversity. After the Act was repealed only the richest and strongest brewers were in a position to take best advantage of the new freedom and the number of breweries never rose much above 700. Soon even that seemed a distant dream as mergers and takeovers concentrated the industry in fewer and fewer hands, until by 1978 there were just 89 breweries in the entire country.

Meanwhile, a movement had arisen that was to be the salvation of US beer—home brewing. Spurred on by the increasing blandness and similarity of mass-market beers or 'Budmilloors' (as the generic product is sometimes called), beer lovers started brewing their own and demonstrating via organisations like the American Homebrewers Association (AHA) that there were plenty of them and they were articulate. People like Charlie Papazian, who was one of the founders of the AHA, preached the doctrine of diversity and people listened. States began passing laws allowing small breweries to be set up and in 1977 the New Albion Brewing Company was established in Sonoma, California, the first new micro-brewery to be set up in the United States in perhaps 100 years. Fritz Maytag took over the Anchor Brewing Company and re-introduced thousands of Americans to one of the country's few unique styles, Steam Beer, a lager–ale hybrid. A businessman and beer lover called Koch decided he wanted to brew a beer of a quality that could compete with the best from Europe. He formulated a recipe and had it brewed under contract by the Pittsburgh Brewing Company. He called it Samuel Adams Boston Lager after the famous founding father, and it was at once accepted as one of the world's great beers.

Now there are more than 800 breweries in the United States brewing a greater variety of beers than any other country in the world—even Belgium. European brewers may at times look on them with disdain as clumsy amateurs but, at their best, these new brewers are producing superb beers. More importantly, they are reminding us that beer is not just a factory product to be used to slake a thirst after a football game but can be and often is as fine, complex and well-crafted a drink as the greatest of wines. Once again the New World has come to the rescue of the Old.

The great beer styles: lagers and pilseners

Traditionally, beers are divided into two basic classes: ales and lagers. The division is by no means an arbitrary one but is based on the way beers are made and, in particular, on how they are fermented. Beers that are brewed using top-fermenting yeasts are broadly classified as ales; those brewed with bottom-fermenters as lagers. Yet, within these two broad categories there are a huge number of further divisions, usually depending on variables like the strength, bitterness or colour of the finished beer.

3 Lagers

The vast majority of the beer consumed in the world today comes under the general heading of lager. The name comes from brewing practice in Bavaria. No doubt because of the troubled times of the Middle Ages and the situation of Bavaria as a meeting place of East and West, Bavarians tended to build their towns around rocky outcrops which could be easily fortified against passing marauders or would-be invaders—the citadels of Bamberg and Nuremberg are perfect examples. The sedimentary structure of the terrain and the porosity of these rocks made them natural retainers of water and the brewers of those times used that water in their brewing. They also were able to cut out extensive caves from the soft but firm sandstone and nowadays those rocks are honeycombed with caverns. In recent times they were used as effective air-raid shelters but in earlier years they came in handy for a more peaceful purpose—storing beer. In the days before refrigeration, brewing generally stopped in the summer months; in fact, as early as 1553, summer brewing was banned in Bavaria. But of course, drinking, far from stopping in the summer, increased enormously. So enough beer had to be stored in the winter months to last through the summer. The caves, with their relatively constant temperatures, proved ideal for that. Over time, the brewers discovered that long-term storage at low temperatures had a beneficial effect on the beer, allowing it to clarify as the yeast dropped out and to stabilise and become smoother in texture as well as develop its own carbonation. The German word for 'to store' or 'to put away' is *lagern*, so beers made with this technique became generally known as lagers.

Great efforts used to be made to keep the caves as cold as possible and huge sinks were cut into the rocks to store ice all the year round. In fact the temperatures in the caves tended to be (and still are) not much lower than around 5°C (36°F) in the winter, even though it might be below zero (32°F) outside.

It was also discovered that conducting the primary fermentation at relatively low temperatures, around 10°C (50°F) as compared with the 18°C (65°F) that was common before, produced a beer with a cleaner finish and favoured yeasts that dropped out to the bottom of the fermenter rather than rising to the top. Thus lagers are also known as bottom-fermented beers.

With the advent of refrigeration, it was no longer necessary to have cold caves to store your beer—and storage temperatures could easily be lowered to below zero (32°F) for even greater stability and clarification—although this last became less important with advances in filtration technology. Even so the technique, with its inherent advantages of stability, spread rapidly first through Europe then the world. Nowadays most of the world's beers are pale golden lagers, both because lager brewing is more controllable, as it does not depend on outside temperatures, and also because lightly flavoured, pale beers clearly appeal to a wider cross-section of the public.

The classic picture of a lager is a pale gold, sparkling beer of around 5 per cent alcohol by volume, fairly lightly hopped and served chilled. However, the first lagers were actually dark beers, because maltsters had not yet devised a way of kilning the grain without also toasting it. That was a breakthrough that came in nearby Bohemia and resulted in the creation of pilsener, the single most popular beer style of them all.

CHAPTER 4

Pilseners

The town of Plzen in the Czech Republic bears the most famous name in beer. But it was almost an accident that led to its fame. In the early years of the nineteenth century the townsfolk of Plzen (*Pilsen* in German), fed up with the low-quality beer their local breweries were producing, banded together to build a new city brewery called Mestansky Pivovar (Burghers' Brewery), later changed to Plzensky Pradroj, the name it still bears. At the same time they hired a German brewer, Joseph Groll, well versed in the Bavarian techniques of bottom-fermentation. Groll's unique recipe, brewed in 1842, using a new product from the local maltsters—a malt kilned at a low enough temperature not to colour it significantly—proved an immediate success. Its golden colour was a marvel and, in a time when glass was becoming more affordable and more in demand for drinking vessels, must have looked spectacularly more brilliant than the old dark beers. Whatever the reasons, it struck a chord with drinkers and proved such a runaway winner that brewers all over Europe started to produce their own versions of the style. The original is still brewed in Pilsen and sold in most parts of the world under its German name of Pilsner Urquell. It is slightly darker than most of its imitators, tending almost towards amber, and is quite highly hopped with another classic product of Bohemia, Zatec or Saaz hops, whose low bitterness combined with the soft water of the area, at best imparts an intense but relatively soft and easy-to-take bitterness to the beer. Some recent samples, however, have shown a tendency to more astringency than they used to have.

FIGURE 4.1
Saaz (Zatec) hops
HOP VARIETIES EUROPEAN GROWN, JOH. BARTH & SOHN, NUREMBERG

FIGURE 4.2
Hop growing and harvesting in the Saaz (Zatec) region, Bohemia (Czech Republic)
THE HOP ATLAS 1994, P. 207, JOH. BARTH & SOHN, NUREMBERG

German pilseners

Despite some pockets of resistance, the neighbouring Germans were quick to take up pilsener and now it is the single most popular style in a country where beer styles proliferate. There are more breweries in Germany than in any other country on earth and almost every city and even town has its pilsener brewery. A few of them have expanded to become national brands but most serve only their local area. German brewers are still bound by the old Bavarian purity law, the *Reinheitsgebot*, so they cannot use adjuncts to lighten the body and colour of their beers; nevertheless, in general, German pilseners tend to be paler and lighter-bodied than the original Czech version. There are definite variations among them, although they all fall within a fairly narrow band. This can even be seen among the popular national brands where some, like Jever, König and Bitburger, emphasise hoppy bitterness and others, like Becks and Warsteiner, lean more towards the malt flavours. Within these limits the beers are usually well balanced, clean and refreshing.

The traditional methods of brewing pilsener, or 'pils' as it is almost invariably called in Germany, are gradually giving way to more simple and efficient methods. Thus the old decoction mash, which involved taking part of the mash out of the mash tun, boiling it and returning it to the tun in order to raise the temperature of the whole mash, appears to be steadily dying out in the north of the country—although the Bavarians, and particularly the smaller brewers, still hold fast to the belief that is the best way to go. Even fermentation practice, almost sacred territory to lager brewers, is far from immune to change. At the big, ultra-modern Warsteiner brewery in the quiet little town of Warstein, a little to the east of the great Rhineland conurbations, a quiet revolution is going on that worries some more traditional brewers. At Warstein, they ferment at the heretical temperature of 15°C (60°F), then lager for only 10 days at around 0 to −2°C (32 to 28°F). This is almost instant brewing by German standards, where lagering times of a month or more are not uncommon and primary fermentation temperatures are usually well below 10°C (50°F). However, the Warsteiner brewers clearly believe their yeast can cope with these huge temperature variations without losing its lager characteristics. The fact that Warsteiner is the single biggest brand in Germany neither supports nor refutes this contention, for much of Warsteiner's success has come from aggressive and innovative marketing and extensive sponsorship campaigns. However, the proof of the pudding is in the tasting, and certainly one would not suspect Warsteiner had been brewed by anything but the standard lager procedure.

Running counter to this trend to modernisation is a move to recapture the past that has seen some small breweries, like the wonderful Pinkus Müller in Münster, prosper, and a range of micro-breweries spring up all over the country, many inspired by the work of the late Otto Binding, a member of the same family that owned the Binding brewery of Frankfurt. This brewery has now, by a process of

FIGURE 4.3
The Warsteiner brewery in Sauerland, Germany
WARSTEINER

FIGURE 4.4
Inside the high-tech Warsteiner brewery in Sauerland, Germany
WARSTEINER

expansion and takeover, emerged as the biggest in Germany. Otto Binding wanted to go back to the beer of his youth and started brewing on a small scale at his Kleines Eltviller Brauhaus in the small Rhineland town of Eltville, using organically grown ingredients and pure mountain water. He also helped other breweries start up similar operations with the result that breweries like Lammsbräu in Neumarkt, north of Munich, produce a range of superb beers, some of them unfiltered. There is even an Otto Binding offshoot in Australia—Scharer's Little Brewery in the town of Picton just outside Sydney.

A German Pils is highly carbonated and, with its all-malt structure and cool fermentation, it carries and sustains a big, tightly matted head. Where it is taken seriously, pouring a pils is almost a ritual in itself, with the glass being topped up bit by bit as the head soars then recedes. I was told by one barmaid that my pils would take seven minutes to pour. I suggested she had better start straight away!

North European pilseners

The bottom-fermenting lager technique was quick to spread to Holland, Belgium and Scandinavia. Indeed, Carlsberg of Denmark was the first organisation to isolate and propagate a single yeast culture, hence the generic name once used for all bottom-fermenting yeasts, *Saccharomyces carlsbergensis*. The northern brewers took the German style of light pilsener even further, unhindered by any constraints on adjuncts. Carlsberg, which is officially a charity (unlike most of the outlets that sell its beer!), is probably the classic example of the style—very pale, very fresh, with a slightly floral hop aroma and a relatively mild bitterness in the finish.

In neighbouring Holland, the great achievement by the brewers and marketers of Heineken has been to create the first genuine world beer. Heineken is the second-biggest brewer in the world after the United State's Anheuser-Busch but it is by far the world's biggest beer exporter. There are few places where you will not find a Heineken—although, in many cases, it is a beer brewed under licence and significantly different from the original. British Heineken is a case in point, a vastly inferior beer to the Dutch original. However, where you can find the original Dutch-brewed product it stands out as a kind of benchmark for beers. You could say that if a beer is better than a Heineken, it's a good beer; if it isn't, it isn't.

Heineken is also notable for popularising the use of green bottles for beer in the face of the fact that green glass is not particularly effective in protecting the product from damage caused by light rays. Beer left exposed to the light can develop nasty flavours, described by Americans as 'skunky' and by the British as 'catty'. Either way, they are not pleasant. Heineken has from time to time claimed that it uses a special kind of green glass to protect the beer but it is also possible that most of the protection comes from specially treated hop extracts known as 'tetras', which are also used when beer is bottled in clear glass, another growing world trend.

Pilsener styles around the world

Northern pilseners have also spawned distant relatives in parts of the world not usually associated with a beer tradition. Latin, wine-drinking countries like Italy and Spain are still quite substantial consumers of beer and Italy's Peroni and Dreher (the latter named after one of the great brewing pioneers) are well-known in many parts of the world as high-quality brews very much in the German/north European style.

In Asia, the most notable beer-producing and -drinking nation is Japan where Asahi, Kirin, Sapporo and Suntory are the major producers of high-quality lagers in this style. In fact the Japanese are devoted users of the finest (and most expensive) aroma hops to flavour their beer, which probably gives them a better, or at least more easily documented, claim to quality than some more prestigious European names.

Most Asian countries now produce beers in this style. For instance, despite being a largely Muslim country, Malaysia has a thriving beer industry with names like Heineken, Tuborg and Carlsberg all in evidence, while a local brewer produces the classic Malaysian/Singaporean beer, Tiger. These beers tend to be surprisingly malty considering the tropical humidity of the climate in which they are consumed.

Indonesia is famous for its Bintang, which was developed in conjunction with Heineken; Thailand has the very hoppy Singha, another big user of aroma hops; and in China you will find perhaps the best Asian beers of them all, Beijing Beer and Xing Tao. There's even a pilsener-style beer brewed on the tiny South Sea islands of Western Samoa, named Vailima after the house in Samoa where the author of *Treasure Island*, Robert Louis Stevenson, ended his days.

Not surprisingly, the mainly Muslim Middle East is not a noted centre of beer drinking, but Africa has its share of pilsener-style beers, brought to the dark continent by white settlers, ranging from the products of the big South African Breweries to the famous Tusker Lager which has soothed the throat of many a coffee planter in Kenya.

Back across the Atlantic, the other notable beer nation, other than the United States, is Mexico, which has a tradition (dating back to the time when it was ruled by a Hapsburg emperor) of tawny, malty Vienna-style lagers, and a more recent explosion of trendy pale imitation pilseners like Corona. The latter for some reason, was taken up in the United States, where it became the custom to drink it with a segment of lime stuck in the neck of the bottle.

American light

The United States is the biggest single beer market in the world, though its per capita consumption is relatively modest compared with Germany and the Czech Republic. It also boasts the biggest-selling brand, Budweiser from Anheuser-Busch. The name derives from a fact-finding trip the company's founder Adolph Busch made to Bohemia in the late nineteenth century. In the town of Ceske Budejovice he found a beer he thought would make a good model for the beers he wanted to brew in the US. The town's German name is *Budweis* so the beer became Budweiser, known affectionately by Americans as 'Bud' (and sent up in the cartoon series *The Simpsons* as 'Duff'). The beer Busch encountered in Bohemia would have had only a token resemblance to Budweiser as brewed today in the United States, and in fact there is still a Bohemian Budweiser, known throughout Europe as Budweiser Budvar, which is probably considerably closer to the original in its rich maltiness and firm bitterness.

The Anheuser-Busch Budweiser is not without hoppiness but it is concentrated in the nose and the early palate and there is little bitterness in the finish. In fact, if there were, the beer would probably be badly out of balance because it is unashamedly brewed with adjuncts other than malt (notably sugars derived from rice) in order to give it the lightness of body and flavour necessary to appeal to the American palate. That it appeals to the American taste is inarguable, but the question remains whether that taste arose through public demand or whether Bud and the beers produced by its competitors, notably Miller's and Coors, created it rather in the way McDonald's created a demand for bland hamburgers and French fries. American light, as the style is generically known, has taken pilsener about as far as possible in the direction of gentle inoffensiveness. It probably deserves a place among the great beer styles of the world simply because it sells so much, but it's hard to see any other reason for considering it.

Canadian lagers

Similar in style to their US neighbours, mainstream Canadian lagers tend to be slightly less floral and more malty, although they are still light-bodied and rather bland by European standards. Typical examples are Labatt's Blue, Moosehead and Molson.

Australian and New Zealand lagers

Most nations are highly chauvinistic about their beers, assuming they are the best in the world and that others' are no better than the waste products of cats. In the case of the great brewing lands of Germany, Belgium and Britain, and probably Holland and Scandinavia, this is perhaps understandable, although hardly broad-minded or sensible. In the case of Australia it is simple insular ignorance. Australia has rationalised its industry down to a duopoly with the two major brewers, Foster's and Lion Nathan, permanently at war over a few disputed percentage points of sales penetration, a very small import section and one or two tiny brewers trying to get a minuscule share of a fraction of a per cent. The result is, not surprisingly, that Australian mainstream beers are tailored not so much to please as many tastes as possible but to try to offend no one. The result of this, combined with a tradition of using adjuncts to eke out and lighten the product, and the almost exclusive use of one variety of high-alpha hops (Pride of Ringwood), which is in use virtually nowhere else, is one of the least interesting beer styles in the world. Australian beers, whether light or dark, often start well, particularly on a hot summer's day, but the fresh lightness of taste does not hold up and the drinker is left with a sweetish sourness barely tempered by a mild dose of hopping.

Most of the beer sold and drunk in Australia comes under the general heading of pilsener-derived lager, but Australian brewers have put their own particular stamp on the style. For various reasons, most of them probably economic, Australian brewers have tended to use a large percentage of adjuncts (fermentable material other than malted barley) in their brewing. Since Australia produces huge amounts of cane sugar, the adjuncts most commonly used are by-products of that. Cane sugar imparts little flavour to a beer and tends to thin out the body; so it's not surprising that Australian lagers have tended to be mild-tasting, light-bodied and very similar in flavour profile right across the country. There is nothing that could be called a regional style, although the oddly named XXXX ('Fourex' to its devotees) from subtropical Queensland, and Cascade from cool temperate Tasmania, are a little more distinctive than the others in their use of hops. The most famous of Australian beers is Foster's Lager, a perfect

Figure 4.6
An oil painting of the historic Cascade brewery by Haughton Fowest 1886
The Hop Atlas 1994, p. 261, Joh. Barth & Sohn, Nuremberg

example of the 'offend no one' philosophy which seems to have succeeded so well with Australian drinkers. Sceptics, however, might well wonder whether the continual decline in beer drinking in Australia does not have some connection with the quality of the product being offered.

A range of premium beers has been growing steadily over the past few years, varying the standard product with just a touch more hopping and a little more malt (and charging considerably more for the privilege), but none has totally escaped the straitjacket of the Australian tradition. Lion's once all-malt Hahn Premium was relaunched a couple of years ago in a more populist, sugar-adjuncted form but retained most of its character; while James Boag and Cascade Premium, both from Tasmania, make the best of traditional Australian hops and malt. None has yet managed to shake off the stranglehold on the premium market of Crown Lager, which appears to be little more than a Foster's with a little polishing.

New Zealand has been considerably more successful in the premium field with Lion Nathan's Steinlager but in standard lagers the picture is not very different from Australia. New Zealand lagers are similar in body to those of Australia but tend to finish with more sweetness, despite the fact that New Zealand grows some of the most bitter hops in the world.

5 Non-pilsener lager styles

FIGURE 5.1

Spaten lager, Munich, Germany

SPATEN

Munich helles

The brewers of Bavaria, despite being adjacent to Bohemia, were slow to adopt the paler style of beer, partly because they liked their dark Dunkel lager and partly because their water supplies were relatively hard and they found it difficult to use the kind of heavy hopping required for a pilsener without turning out a beer that was just too aggressively bitter. Thanks largely to the work of Gabriel Sedlmayr, brewmaster at the Spaten brewery in Munich, an alternative style of pale lager was developed in Munich, known simply as 'helles' from the German word *hell*, meaning 'light' or 'bright'. Although most of the big Bavarian brewers make their own versions of pils, it is helles that is the trademark brew of Bavaria. It is brewed in much the same way as a pilsener but with extra care taken to keep the finished product as smooth as possible. At some breweries they even wet the malt before grinding in order to prevent the grain husks from splitting and releasing tannins into the mash. This obsession with smoothness continues throughout the brewing process. A high proportion of the hops, which often go into the boil in two or three dosages, consists of high-quality (and high-priced) aroma hops from the nearby hop fields of the Hallertau. The mash and hot wort are carefully handled to prevent oxidisation, fermentation is done at around 8–9°C (46–48°F), followed by a four-week lagering period going down below zero (32°F) before the beer is filtered to a sparkling brightness. The result is one of the world's greatest beer styles, a golden, mouth-filling, malty brew that finishes with a pleasantly rounded bitterness. Each helles brewery—and there are hundreds of them in Bavaria—turns out its own version of the style; the original, Spaten, is particularly smooth; the most famous internationally, Löwenbräu, a little more pungently hoppy; Augustiner and Ayinger gloriously malty. All are beautiful beers and there are few pleasanter ways of spending time than with a half-litre (or more) in front of you.

Dortmunder export

Dortmund brews more beer than any other city in Germany, although it does not have a particularly large number of breweries—about nine appears to be the figure at the time of writing, although that is changing all the time as amalgamations proceed. Since it is not one of the country's largest cities, much of this output is exported both within Germany and to the world. The Dortmund brewers produce plenty of pilsener but they have also put their own spin on the pilsener style by producing a beer with a similarly clean body but slightly more colour and tending more to the malty end of the taste spectrum. Originally this was made slightly stronger than the norm, as usual with beers that have to travel, but nowadays Dortmunder export—which can only be produced in Dortmund—is usually brewed at around the average 5 per cent alcohol by volume.

Vienna, märzen and oktoberfest

The vienna style originated in Vienna, Austria, where it was made famous by the great brewer Anton Dreher. From this style, the neighbouring Bavarians developed their own version, which is known as either märzen or oktoberfest. All three styles have one thing in common—they are amber lagers using the more highly kilned Vienna and Munich malts and giving a strong emphasis on malt flavour. In terms of alcohol, vienna is the lightest of them, around 5% alc/vol (4% alc/wt); märzen and oktoberfest are essentially the same beer style, brewed for the same purpose but under two different names.

Märzen gets its name because it was brewed in March; however, the purpose of brewing in March was to store it in the caves until October at which time the casks would be broached for the great Oktoberfest celebration. To make sure the celebration went with a bang, this was a strong beer (6% alc/vol, 5% alc/wt). Märzen/oktoberfest versions of the style have almost entirely superseded the original vienna version but, to compensate, some of them are now lower in alcoholic strength than they

FIGURE 5.4

Oktoberfest celebrations, 1995

LÖWENBRÄU AG, MUNICH, GERMANY

used to be and so are, in fact, nearer to the original vienna style. Being seasonal beers it is not always possible to find them outside the festival times.

Samuel Adams Boston Lager

In recent years, a new wave of beer connoisseurship has spread all across the United States and with it have sprung up hundreds of micro-breweries brewing just about every beer style known to humankind. Mostly they brew traditional European, British and Belgian styles but often modified according to their own tastes and the likes and dislikes of their customers. Probably the most important of these has been the Boston Brewing Company which, in the mid 1980s, produced Samuel Adams Boston Lager, an all-malt beer that has strong echoes of the vienna style in its dark amber-brown colour and malty palate but uses hops in a much more distinctive way to give a strong hop flavour and an instantly noticeable hop aroma that lingers

enjoyably all the way down the glass. In effect, by blending the characteristics of the pilsener and vienna styles, the brewers of Samuel Adams have created a new style of their own.

Munich dunkel

The style of beer popular in Bavaria before the arrival of pale malts was the dunkel, or dark, lager, and this is still a highly popular style in and around Munich. Most breweries produce their own version with the ingredients varying according to the size of the enterprise and how much of it is devoted to this particular style. A brewery specialising in helles but producing a small amount of dunkel will mash with mainly pale malt, adding darker malts like crystal (caramel) and chocolate to achieve the required darkness of colour. On the other hand, if a brewery specialises in dark beers it will more likely use a base malt like Munich malt, which is kilned to a slightly darker colour than pale malt, and get the necessary colour in the beer from that. A dunkel bears a superficial resemblance to an ale because the strong flavour of the dark malts tends to override any subtle flavour differences created by the yeast. However, the fruity esters found in a top-fermented beer are or should be absent from this style, whose characteristics are smoothness and a chocolatey finish tempered with moderate hopping. Most of the Bavarian brewers have their own version of the style with slight variations from place to place. Spaten's Dunkel Export and Augustiner's Dunkel Volbier are considered classics of the style, although there are so many small breweries in Bavaria that it would be unwise to be too dogmatic about that. Löwenbräu is one of the few Bavarian breweries actively exporting the style to distant parts of the world.

Bock and doppelbock

There are two stories that account for the name 'bock'. One holds that the name came simply from the fact that the beer was strong and some labels had a billygoat (*Bock* in German) pictured on them. But the most popular theory is that the name derives from the town of Einbeck in Lower Saxony, north of Bavaria, which was famous as a quality brewing centre long before Bavaria itself and exported its beer all over Germany. In the Bavarian accent, Einbeck became Einbock, so the beer became 'bock'. Bock beers are lagers which can be either pale or dark but are usually very strong (6–7% alt/vol, 5–6%alc/wt) and, not surprisingly, considering the brewers are unable to use anything but malt in them, distinctly malty. Even stronger, and even maltier, are doppelbocks, distinctively darker beers with an enormous kick in them provided by an alcohol content of 8–12% alc/vol (6.5–9.5% alc/wt). One of the first known doppelbocks was produced by a monastery brewery and called Salvator ('Saviour'); since then it has been a tradition that doppelbocks should have names ending in 'ator', although that is not compulsory. So the very strong doppelbock of the city of Kulmbach is known as Kulminator and there are

FIGURE 5.5

The Löwenbräu brewery in Munich, Bavaria, Germany, showing the control room and the old copper brew kettles and (below) the holding tanks.
LAURIE STRACHAN

FIGURE 5.6
LAURIE STRACHAN

others called Celebrator, and so on. There's even one called Terminator, which, if not treated with respect, will do you the kind of damage Arnold Schwarzenegger does to his foes. EKU of Kulmbach produces a brew called simply EKU 28, which indicates that its original gravity figure, measured on the balling scale universally used in Europe, is at least 28. That figure would give a final alcohol per volume rating of around 12% alc/vol (9.5% alc/wt). Because of the huge amounts of malt required to reach these strengths, these beers are very rich and cloying on the palate, giving them the feel almost of liqueurs and making them drinkable in only very small quantities (which is perhaps just as well).

Eisbock

Eisbock is a rare specialty that is difficult to find nowadays. It is simply a strong beer given a final treatment to make it even stronger. It is frozen until clumps of ice form. Since water freezes at a higher temperature than alcohol, these clumps are mostly water. They are removed and the resulting beer is left just that little bit stronger.

Steinbiere

Steinbiere is another historical curiosity that has been revived in the town of Altenmünster west of Munich. It is said to date from the time when brewing kettles were made of wood and therefore could not be put on the fire to heat them. Instead, the brewers built a huge fire and heated rocks on it. The rocks were then plunged into the wort, bringing it up to the boil. In the course of this they would acquire a coating of caramelised malt. During fermentation, these same rocks would be immersed in the wort, releasing a rich caramel flavour into the brewing beer. The story has never really rung true, for it is hard to imagine boiling an entire wort just by dropping hot rocks in it. However, the technique may well have been used simply as a flavour enhancer or perhaps as a means of adding a sudden extra charge of heat to the kettle.

Kellerbier

Yet another Bavarian specialty, kellerbier is, as its name suggests, a beer served directly from the cellars of inns and pubs. Like many beers it is given a secondary fermentation but in this case most of the carbon dioxide is

FIGURE 5.8
Matthias Trum, brewmaster at Heller Brewery,
Bamberg, Germany
LAURIE STRACHAN

FIGURE 5.9
Beech logs for smoking Heller rauchmalz
LAURIE STRACHAN

allowed to dissipate so the beer is served fairly flat. It seems to be growing in popularity in small pub breweries where it saves time and effort in the carbonation and packaging.

Rauchbier

Though apparently one of the more unusual styles of beer found in Germany, rauchbier is actually a quite logical development of old brewing and, more particularly, malting technology. The name literally means 'smoke beer'; it is an ancient style that has never quite died out and has been revived with great success in recent years. It derives from the way malt used to be kilned over beech logs, rather in the way Scottish malt is kilned over peat fires before being mashed and turned into malt whisky. Rauchbier producers, like the famous Heller brewery in the Franconian city of Bamberg, usually have their own small maltings where they apply this old process. The beer itself is brewed like a dunkel lager with a double decoction mash and bottom-fermentation. The smoky kilning provides both the dark colour and the smoky tang that gives the beer its unique flavour and turns it into something quite

FIGURE 5.10
Sign outside Schlenkerla tavern, Bamberg
LAURIE STRACHAN

different from, and altogether more interesting than, the standard dunkel. Hops are relatively unimportant in this style as the smoky aroma and flavour tends to override them. Heller's rauchbier, combined with an earthy, homely atmosphere, has turned the Schlenkerla tavern in Bamberg into one of the best-known pubs in Germany and a must-stop for any visitor to that historic and beautifully preserved city.

Steam Beer

A style that is unique to the United States (American light is clearly a pilsener derivative), and still being brewed, is Steam Beer. Steam Beer is a product of United States' most distinguished small brewing company, Anchor of San Francisco, which holds the name as a trademark. Essentially it is made by a hybrid of the lager and ale brewing methods, which dates to the years in California before refrigeration was developed. After boiling, the hot wort was pumped into wide, flat trays like the 'coolships' still in use in some European breweries today. However, once the wort was cool enough the yeast was pitched into it there in the coolship, whereas European practice had always been to move it to deeper fermentation tanks. The yeast itself was a bottom-fermenter but fermentation was done at ambient temperatures. The result

was a beer with some of the characteristics of both an ale and a lager, richly malty and well flavoured. In fact some authorities classify this as an ale rather than a lager—but the jury is still out on that one.

Dry and light beers

The idea of the 'dry' beer seems to have originated in Japan (although I can't for the life of me think why). This is a beer, usually a lager, in which both mashing and fermentation techniques are tailored to produce a brew that will ferment out further than the normal product. The result is a beer with a very thin, very light body and a low level of sweetness. It is not necessarily particularly bitter but does give a sensation of dryness on the tongue, rather in the manner of a well-attenuated white wine. Light (or lite) beers can either be beers with a low alcohol content or beers with a modified carbohydrate content so they contain fewer calories. Dry and light beers are difficult for the home brewer to emulate—and scarcely worth the trouble.

The great beer styles: ales, the original beers

The word 'ale' is ancient, but not nearly as ancient as the drink it describes. It is often used to casually describe any beer, as in the expression 'a cleansing ale', and there are all sorts of beers which confusingly carry the label—like Australia's Cascade Pale Ale and Castlemaine Bitter Ale. However, ale has a much more exact definition than that. Beer historian Terry Foster, in his *Doctor Foster's Book of Beer*, stated that the correct use of the word 'ale' is to describe beers made before the introduction of hops. Nowadays, however, it is generally agreed that ales are simply beers fermented by the traditional top-fermentation system, which was the only system in use before lagers came on the scene and stole their empire. Up until the mid-nineteenth century, when Bavarian brewers made their trial-and-error discoveries about lagering—and then how that encouraged the growth and use of yeasts that dropped to the bottom of the fermenter when they had done their work instead of floating to the top—every beer was an ale. Even after that discovery, ales were still the ruling class because you needed special conditions, mainly plentiful cold storage areas, in which to ferment and lager the beer. In most places that just wasn't possible until the invention of refrigeration by Linde and its application to the brewing process by Gabriel Sedlmayr in the Spaten brewery in Munich in 1873. After that, the benefits of lager brewing and the stability it brought to beer encouraged brewers all over Europe to adopt it.

However, in just a few places, ale held out against the golden tide and in those enclaves it has continued to thrive, although at times it has been under severe threat. What's more, although ales retain only a tiny fraction of the world beer market, their devotees consider that fraction to be by far the most interesting part of the entire spectrum of beer. It is also the most widely, and wildly, varied part of that world. The range of styles is theoretically close to infinite and in reality still quite astonishing; in one country alone, Belgium, there is a wider range of styles of beer than in most of the rest of the world put together. Belgium and Britain are the last two remaining national strongholds of ale, but the style has strong and well-established domains in the heart of lagerland itself, Germany.

British ales

Real ale

Real ale is not a style of beer, but is rather a definition the Campaign for Real Ale (CAMRA) created in the late 1960s. It has as much to do with the way beer is packaged as how it is made. Traditional British beer had always been served 'live', that is, with the yeast still working in it and keeping it lively, and with no top pressure in the cask. The beer was, and is, brought up from the cellar to the taps by 'beer machines', simple lift pumps that do not depend on the beer being pressurised. The trouble with this system from the publicans' and brewers' points of view was that it required a fair degree of expertise in the handling of the beer at the pub. In the first place, the pub needed to possess a properly cool cellar, and in the second, the cellerman had to be an expert in judging just when the beer had reached the point where it was ready to be served. If the cellerman was not up to the job, the result could be low-quality beer reaching the customer.

Naturally, the brewers were unhappy about this and their answer was to pasteurise and filter their beer so that fermentation was complete before it went into the keg. Pasteurised beer needs to be protected from the air or it will quickly oxidise and become undrinkable, so it had to be packaged under pressure in metal kegs. These could then be sent out to pubs that needed to do no more than bang in a tap and attach the keg to a CO_2 cylinder, then start serving it. The need for expert cellaring was removed. Unfortunately, this process changed the character of the beer completely. From being a living, fermenting beer it became inert and lifeless and the CO_2 needed to preserve and dispense it from the pressure taps gave it a fizzy, gassy character that obscured the fine qualities of the malt and hops. The frontrunner in the keg invasion was the

FIGURE 6.1

Traditional transport method

FULLER SMITH & TURNER PLC, LONDON

FIGURE 6.2

Traditional English pub

FULLER SMITH & TURNER PLC, LONDON

now-infamous Watney's Red Barrel, but other major breweries quickly followed suit.

The people who founded CAMRA could see that if this trend continued indefinitely, the traditional British pint would disappear and be replaced with fizzy keg beers. So they defined traditionally packaged beers as 'real ale' and set out to raise public awareness of what was happening. History shows they were highly successful and now most major breweries, while still producing keg beer, also produce one or more traditional real ales—whether they are bitters, milds, old ales or anything else. In an ideal world, CAMRA would no doubt prefer British beers to be brewed without adjuncts, following a kind of unofficial *Reinheitsgebot*, but in the real world, the practice in Britain is so much bound up with the use of various additions other than malt that this is probably an impossible dream—and in any case, at their best, British beers are already of very high quality.

Though the real ale battle appears to have been won, CAMRA is still a very useful and influential organisation. It has been described as the world's most successful consumer organisation and it still acts as a watchdog on beer quality in Britain as well as organising opposition to the ever-increasing 'rationalisation' of the brewing industry in Britain and Ireland. Its regular publications, like the *Good Beer Guide* and the *Good Pub Guide*, are invaluable for anyone who lives in or visits Britain and wants to sample the best this great brewing region can offer.

Bitter

English bitter is probably the best known style of ale in the world today—though in fact it is more a range of styles than a single entity. There is a bitter for virtually all seasons and for nearly all palates. Ideally a bitter, to live up to its name, should have strong hop character and bitterness but even that aspect of the style cannot be taken absolutely for granted. Colour also varies enormously, from those that are pale and almost lager-like to examples that have the dark brown tang of a brown ale.

There are basically three levels of bitter—in ascending order of alcoholic strength they are ordinary bitter (3.5–4% alc/vol, 2.8–3.2% alc/wt), special bitter (4–5%, 3.2–4%) and extra-special bitter (5–6%, 4–5%). In practice, however, it can be very difficult to work out which beer fits into which category—certainly the names they go under are only occasionally an accurate guide. The thing about bitter of course is that it hardly matters. The British tradition of 'muddling through' has worked very well in this case, and one of the great joys of drinking beer in Britain is working your way through all the permutations. One hundred years ago there were many hundreds of small breweries all over Britain, each producing their own particular style of bitter. Today with the brewing universe contracting rapidly, the great majority of these beers has vanished, swallowed up in a seemingly never-ending series of amalgamations and takeovers. No doubt some of these might well have been rather ordinary products and it's possible that this consolidation has, to some extent, been a case of survival of the fittest but, however you look at it, the drinker's choice has diminished greatly.

However, there are still a host of wonderful bitters to be found in Britain, and particularly in England, which is the home of the style. For instance, the London area still boasts two of the finest British breweries, Fuller's, Smith and Turner, and Young's. Fuller's London Pride and Extra Special Bitter are almost legendary among lovers of English beer, gloriously rich and mouth-filling and both beautifully balanced; London Pride fruity yet dry-finishing, the stronger ESB malty and satisfying. Young's is particularly famous for its Special Bitter, a paler example of the style with the emphasis firmly in the hops in a pungently bitter finish.

Though there is no definite regional pattern to English bitters, further north, in Yorkshire, the beers often tend to become darker and more malty. Classic examples are the Old Brewery Bitter from the still-independent Samuel Smith's of Tadcaster in Yorkshire, not particularly dark but a smoothly malty standard bitter produced in the traditional 'Yorkshire square' fermenters; next door John Smith's, an offshoot of the giant Scottish Courage, uses more modern equipment to produce its excellent, eponymous bitter. The small Theakston's brewery is most renowned for its classic old ale, Old Peculier (yes, that's how they spell it), but also exports its Best Bitter all over the world; while in Leeds, Tetley's uses a modern, stainless-steel version of the Yorkshire square to ferment its successful national brand, Tetley's Bitter. Northern beers also tend to carry more carbonation and more of a head than those from the south.

Across the Pennines in Manchester, Boddington's brew a much paler version of bitter, nearly as light in colour as many lagers. This has been successfully marketed in the 'widget' cans that release nitrogen into the beer at the moment they are opened, creating a smooth, creamy head to top an already polished palate. Interestingly, the version brewed for sale in Britain contains around 4% alc/vol (3.2% alc/wt) while the export version rates at 5% (4%). A darker example is Courage's Director's Bitter, produced at the brewing giant's Bristol plant.

Most of the other big names in British brewing, like Whitbread, Ind Coope Ushers and Vaux, brew bitters—some brew several—and there is a score or more of lesser-known but distinguished names like Adnam's, Greene King, King and Barnes, Marston's, Morland and Shepherd Neame who brew beers well worth tasting. Add to this the output of the new, revivalist micro-breweries that are now dotted around the country and it becomes obvious that bitter is alive and well—and just waiting to be tasted.

Pale ale

Either pale ale is a development of bitter or vice versa. It used to be considered that pale ale was merely bitter in its bottled form, but nowadays many 'pales' are widely on sale on draught and some bitters are bottled and canned, so that is hardly a tenable position. The heartland of pale ale is the Midlands area of England around Burton-on-Trent, where the style was perfected. Despite the name, pale ale is not particularly pale, more a rich amber. It is also usually well hopped and relatively strong as British beers go—between 4.5–5.5% (3.5%–4.5%). A subdivision of this style called India Pale Ale was originally brewed to be transported to India to slake the thirst of the British troops who held the thin red line against the imagined excesses of the orientals. It was therefore produced with a high level of alcohol and a lot of hop bitterness—both aimed at preserving the beer on its long sea voyage through huge ranges of temperature. Nowadays, an India Pale Ale is often hard to distinguish from its stay-at-home cousins; nor, with the general decline in hopping rates in English beers, is the bitterness level as high as it was.

The classic of the pale ale style is Bass from Burton-on-Trent in the southern Midlands of England, one of the great brewing centres of the nineteenth century and still important today. Bass almost sets the standard for pale ale with its amber colour and pleasant hoppiness and is perhaps the best-known and most distinguished of all British beer labels; it is also owner of the world's first trademark, the famous red triangle. Although the bottled Bass that is exported all over the world, with its mild palate and bland finish, seems a far cry from the original, Draught Bass served from the keg is something else, a smooth, elegant tawny ale, while the bottle-conditioned Worthington White Shield, also produced by Bass, is considered by many to be the classic example of a bottled pale ale. However, the style is by no means confined to the Midlands. Many other breweries, in all parts of the country, including Scotland, produce pale ales, with varying degrees of success.

Mild

Mild ale was once very popular in England as the working man's pint. Its low alcoholic strength, mild hopping and pleasantly chocolatey flavour made it easy drinking, in large quantities, after a hard day's manual work. Now, perhaps because of this very association with rude toil, its place has been largely usurped by lager. The two beers could hardly be more different. Whereas lager is pale golden, hoppy (though perhaps not in the case of British lagers) and highly carbonated, mild ale is a flattish dark brown ale with a low hop bitterness. The style with its characteristic use of dark malts was obviously the answer to the age-old problem of brewing a beer with relatively low alcohol but still a reasonable flavour. Roasted malts do not add any fermentables to the brew but if used judiciously, they do add flavour and a pleasantly roasted aroma. The name 'mild' appears to refer to the low level of bitterness compared with the aptly named bitter rather than the fact that the beer is not strong in alcohol; however, most milds are mild in both senses and rate at around 3–3.5% alc/vol (2.4–2.8% alc/wt). Not many brewers now produce milds but Fuller's in London and Boddington's in Manchester, among the major breweries, both produce good examples of the style.

Brown ale

The obvious characteristic of brown ale is its colour but it differs in other ways from bitter. The most obvious is in a lower level of bitterness, more akin to that of a mild but with an alcohol level of around 4.5–5% by volume (3.5–4% alc/wt). It is also more highly carbonated in the northern manner. The north-east of the country, in the Newcastle–Tyneside area, is the heartland of the style, and the most famous example is Newcastle Brown, an old favourite that can be found all over the world. As its name implies, it is a dark brown ale, although usually not quite as dark as a mild.

Irish red ale

A variant on brown ale that has surged in popularity in recent years partly, no doubt, because of the mushrooming of 'Irish Pubs' in every part of the globe. (They can be found in places as far apart as Sydney, Australia, and Düsseldorf, Germany—there are two in that city's Altstadt, almost side by side.) Red ale, like its brown cousin, is a dark beer with a reddish tinge to its colour, as the name implies. It is usually lightly hopped and served on tap under nitrogen pressure, like that other Irish classic Guinness, to give it a thick, creamy head.

Scottish ales

To the casual observer, Scottish beers are scarcely distinguishable from their English relatives but, on closer examination, subtle but important differences become apparent. The most obvious one is the way they are named. Where England has 'bitter' and 'mild', Scotland has 'heavy' and 'light'. This, in itself, is slightly confusing because light, like mild, has always been a darker colour than heavy. There are also two stronger grades, 'export' and 'wee heavy'—this last one a very strong beer, almost a barley wine, which gets its name from being sold in smaller bottles to compensate for its extra strength. However, all that appears to be changing as the

CAMRA revolution sweeps through the British beer world and nowadays you are as likely to find Scottish beers under names like McEwan's 70/- or Belhaven 80/-. These names refer back to history in two ways. The '/-' designation is the old symbol for a shilling, which used to be an integral part of the pounds, shillings and pence structure of the British currency before decimalisation reduced it to merely pounds and pence. A shilling was worth one-twentieth of a pound, or 12 pence, and casks of beer were rated according to their cost in shillings, which equated with their strength in alcohol. Nowadays the figures are completely irrelevant in currency terms but, with the return to traditional concepts that followed CAMRA's successful activities, Scottish brewers have taken to using these old terms as labels for their beer. Thus an ale rated at 70/- would probably be approximately a standard heavy, while the 80/- would be an export.

Perhaps because the country is colder, or more likely because Scottish brewers have never had such close access to hop fields as their southern brethren, Scottish beers have never been quite as bitter as their English equivalents. The typical Scottish heavy has usually been darker than the standard bitter, closer in colour to a brown ale, and has tended to have a strongly malty palate, fermented out to a clean finish without a noticeable hoppiness. Like most things in brewing, however, that seems to be changing a little as independent brewers, large (like Caledonian in Edinburgh) and small (like Harviestoun in Dollar), put more emphasis on the hops than the traditional mass-market brewers like McEwans/Youngers. The once-obscure Belhaven in Dunbar, south of Edinburgh, is now a major player in the Scottish beer market and produces a beautifully balanced 80/- on draught and a canned 60/- known as Belhaven Best, which, despite its low alcohol content of 3.5% alc/vol (2.8% alc/wt), packs an impressive punch of flavour.

Porter

Porter is the Jurassic Park of beers. After a long and successful existence, beginning in the early eighteenth century, it became completely extinct in the country of its birth and has only been revived in the past 20 years. The problem that this leaves us with is that we don't really know exactly how porter looked or tasted. We do know that it was a dark beer of reasonable strength but working out how dark, how strong and how bitter is close to guesswork. The style was originally known by two names, Porter and Entire. The second and probably the earlier of these is thought to have been derived from the fact that it was either a mixture of two or three different beers or of two or three different mashes which, before Entire was devised, were sold separately and often mixed into a blend in the drinker's glass. In the way that its growth mushroomed, spreading rapidly even into the emerging United States (George Washington was fond of the odd glass), porter was the lager of the eighteenth century. The style was developed in London and, as previously stated, one theory holds that it got the name porter because it was the favoured drink of London's porters; another posits that the name became attached to it because when the men from the brewery delivered it they would call out 'Porter!' to announce their arrival.

Over the nineteenth century porter's popularity began to decline in the face of competition from pale ales and bitters and by the 1930s it had disappeared entire (so to speak). We can reasonably assume that it was originally a rich, dark beer with an alcohol level of between 5 and 7%, though there can be little doubt that it would have varied considerably from brewer to brewer. Over the years it seems to have lost its own identity by splitting into two distinct alternative beers, both of them dark—mild at the low-alcohol end and stout at the other. The CAMRA revolution plus the growth of home brewing and pub breweries saw interest in porter revive in the 1960s and '70s and nowadays a growing number of commercial examples of porter can be found in Britain and even more in the United States. Samuel Smith's of Tadcaster in Yorkshire have been brewing and exporting a beautifully rich and well-balanced porter for many years now, as have Anchor in San Francisco, although this latter beer is bottom-fermented and therefore not exactly true to the style.

Stout

Again no one is quite sure where the name 'stout' came from, but in the eighteenth and nineteenth centuries the word generally meant 'strong' rather than 'fat' as it does now, so it may well have been the custom to describe a strong porter as a stout porter. However, stout has evolved into a quite distinct style of its own (with one or two sub-styles). It's even darker than porter, using either black malt or roasted barley or a combination of the two to get its black colour and rich dark flavour, and it tends to have less residual sweetness. The classic dry stout is Ireland's Guinness, a black, almost opaque beer with a palate dominated by the almost coffee-like flavour of roasted barley and a finish of pungent bitterness accented by a deliberate lacing with a slightly soured portion of the beer kept apart for just that purpose. Guinness is also famous for its thick, creamy head in which the drinker is supposed to be able to write his/her name. This is achieved by kegging the beer under nitrogen gas instead of carbon dioxide. This achieves two effects. Unlike CO_2, nitrogen does not dissolve readily into the liquid so the beer does not become highly carbonated. However, as it is poured, the gas forms very small bubbles, much smaller than those formed by CO_2, and so the famous head results. This technique has new been extended to other beers which go under names like Irish Red or Cream Ale. It was also pioneered by Guinness in their canned beers. In this case, the gas is kept in a small compartment inside the can, isolated from the beer; when the ring-pull is opened, this compartment is breached and the gas is allowed into the beer. The result is that same creamy head. Again this highly effective technique has been extended to other beers and is used for other stouts and even bitters like the English Boddington's. Ireland has two other famous brands of stout, Murphy's and Beamish, both subtly different from Guinness, but stouts are now found all over the world. One of the more surprising bastions of the style is Australia, which produces some very fine examples of the style—like Tooth's Sheaf Stout, which is not particularly well known in its own country but is considered a classic in some parts of the world. Other fine stouts come from Cooper's, Southwark and Cascade.

Old ales

Old ales form a rather vague classification somewhere between milds and porters but with certain characteristics, which neither of these possess. Old ales are usually dark in colour and often quite strong in alcohol. Like bitters and other British styles, they vary enormously from one beer to another but they usually have a slightly winey character and are not highly hopped. Classics of the style Old Peculier, brewed by Theakston's of Yorkshire, and the oddly named Old Speckled Hen, brewed by Morland's of Abingdon in Oxfordshire (which calls itself a pale ale but is not nearly hoppy enough to qualify for the style). Many other breweries, large and small, brew their own version of the style, sometimes at very high alcohol rates.

Barley wines

Strong ales overlap into barley wines, which are even stronger and are presumably so named because they are approaching the alcohol content of wines. Like its lager equivalent, the German Doppelbock, barley wine is a very strong beer indeed, usually rating at around 9–12% alc/vol (7.2–9.6% alc/wt). However, unlike the German brews which must conform to the *Reinheitsgebot* and use nothing but malt as fermentable material, barley wines can use adjuncts like cane sugar to mitigate the intense maltiness that would otherwise be inevitable in such a strong brew. Nevertheless the amount of fermentables used in the brewing tends to leave a barley wine with a distinctly sweet flavour, which is balanced off by generous use of hops. If this is done with skill, the effect on the tastebuds is rather like tasting the very essence of beer. The classic barley wine, and the strongest beer brewed in Britain (at 12% alc/vol (9.6% alc/wt)) is the all-malt Thomas Hardy's Ale, brewed by Eldridge Pope in the West Country town of Dorchester, where the famous writer lived and wrote his great series of novels. It was first brewed in 1968 to commemorate the 100th anniversary of Hardy's death and has been produced ever since. Each batch is vintage-dated and expected to be laid down for a few years while it matures.

Strong ales

Related to but not quite as strong as barley wines are the strong ales of Scotland. Best known of these is Fowler's Wee Heavy, a dark, winey, richly flavoured ale with a well-balanced bitterness in the finish that helps it go down well in front of a roaring fire as the chill Scottish winds howl about; Belhaven also makes a good example of the style.

Belgian ales

Although Britain undoubtedly represents the largest remaining stronghold of ales, it is across the North Sea in Belgium that you will find the most remarkable ale culture. Belgium is a small country; you can drive across it in two hours, but if you do, you will miss out on perhaps the most exciting beer country in the world. The lager revolution swept through Belgium as it did in every other European country, and although lagers now account for nearly 75 per cent of the beer consumed in Belgium, the ale brewers of Belgium were never completely defeated. Turning their backs on the new technology and the allure of pale gold pilseners, they went back to the roots of brewing and created a range of beers so astonishingly varied as to almost defy categorisation. There are obvious beer styles in Belgium but only one or two of them conform to any recognisable rules. The rest are a riot of aromas, flavours and colours that go under the general title of *Streekbieren* or 'district beers'. There is something like 400 different ales brewed in Belgium and no two are quite the same. Many of these beers show clear effects of wild yeasts and bacteria of the kind that would have brewers in Germany or the United States recoiling in horror, but that is another time-honoured part of the Belgian brewing tradition and one that reaches its zenith in the spontaneously fermented lambic beers of the Senne Valley near Brussels.

Belgian brewers also extensively use a type of sugar called 'candi' in their brews. This is a sugar that is made by crystallising a concentrated sucrose solution on cotton threads; the slower it is crystallised, the larger the crystals. Although candi comes in two kinds, pale and dark, even the pale version imparts some colour to the beer. Candi is a very pure sugar that is easily dissolved and fermented, but many Belgian brewers believe it aids head retention as well as leaving a distinctive flavour. Also, being highly fermentable it tends to lighten the body of a beer, which makes it particularly useful when you wish to brew the kind of very strong beers favoured by many Belgian ale brewers.

As if to emphasise the dazzling variety of beer styles, every beer is served in its own special glass, even if that specialty is no more than a label. Trappist beers often favour the goblet shape; the staple beer of Antwerp, De Koninck, is served in a round, almost ball-shaped goblet known locally as a *bollockie*. The rich, dark Cuvée de l'Hermitage comes in a low-slung brandy snifter and there is even a thistle-shaped glass for strong Scottish ales, which seem more popular and easier to find in Belgium than in their native land.

Trappist beers

The old traditions were best preserved in the five Trappist monasteries that are dotted around Belgium—in Chimay, Orval, Rochefort, Westmalle and

Westvletteren. Following the tradition of monasteries in the more southern lands of making wines, the monks in these colder outposts, lacking the necessary grapes, took to brewing in the Middle Ages and maintained that tradition through the centuries. After World War II, they re-established their breweries, which had been vandalised by the Germans, who had taken the precious copper for their own war effort, and started brewing again. By the 50's their beers had begun to gain fame throughout the country and others started to copy them. Then in 1962 the Belgian government ruled that only those five monasteries could describe their beer as Trappist beer. That is still the situation today; Trappist beers are a kind of *appellation controlée* similar to the great French wine districts.

Trappist beers vary enormously from one another, although there are two reasonably constant styles, trippel and dubbel. The trippel is the strongest beer the Trappists make (around 9% alc/vol, 7.2% alc/wt) and the style was created by the monks at the monastery of Westmalle near Antwerp. Essentially it is a pale beer, only a little darker than a pilsener, and usually made with pilsener malts supplemented by light candi sugar or glucose. The original Westmalle version has a huge hop aroma and flavour, though not a great deal of bitterness; others tend to be less hoppy. Dubbel is usually a dark amber beer of around 7% alc/vol (5.6% alc/wt) with a pleasantly malty palate.

Not all the Trappist monasteries make this style of beer. Chimay, the biggest of them and perhaps the best known outside Belgium, has a range of brown beers which used to be differentiated only by their crown caps, Red, White and Blue in ascending order of alcohol content. All have that noticeable Belgian wild yeast character although their individual characters are quite different. The top-ranking Chimay Blue (9% alc/vol, 7.2% alc/wt) is also bottled in a 750 ml bottle with a champagne-style cork held on by wire, in which form it is described as Grand Reserve—and is undoubtedly one of the great beers of the world. Another highly individual Trappist beer comes from the Abbey of Orval; unusually this is not a strong beer at just 5% alc/vol (4% alc/wt) but the flavour is highly individual.

Abbey beers

Next in the Belgian pecking order come Abbey beers. These are beers usually in much the same styles as the Trappist beers but brewed by commercial brewers, either in cooperation with actual abbeys like Grimbergen and Affligem, by taking the name of a local abbey or even just by giving the beer a religious-sounding name. There is a huge range of these beers, often following the trippel/dubbel designations, often not.

Specialty beers

If a beer does not fit into any other category it can always be called a specialty beer. As the name implies, this is the most wide-ranging of all the divisions of Belgian ales, covering anything from the darkly malty to pale gold and from dry and sparkling to soft and rich. Perhaps the best known of them all is Duvel, brewed by the Moortgat brewery in Mechelen (Malines). Duvel (the word means 'devil') is a beer of astonishing qualities. It looks almost like a lager but its concentrated flavour and alcoholic strength (8% alc/vol, 6.4 alc/wt%) make sure the resemblance stops there. (In fact, a Belgian friend of mine who used to run a specialty beer cafe in Ghent told me he thought the reason Belgium had had so much trouble with visiting English soccer hooligans was that they drank beers such as Duvel as if they were British lagers of half the strength and got roaring drunk much more quickly than they expected. Well, it's a generous thought but you can take it or leave it.) Duvel has an unusual but exquisite complexity of flavours, which include noble hops, a definite fruitiness almost like a Bavarian wheat beer, a hint of spice and just enough bitterness to finish it all off beautifully.

In fact, if I had to spend my life drinking only one beer I might well choose this one.

It's obviously impossible to categorise specialty beers, and to sample a reasonable range of them you will simply have to go to Belgium, but a few are worth mentioning. Gouden Carolus, again from Mechelen, is an amber-gold ale of rich flavour and just enough hop and wild yeast character to prevent it from cloying; Palm is a lighter variant on the Belgian style with a clean, dry finish; Kwak Pauwel is a richly malty brew with an unusual claim to fame. In at least the specialty cafe Dulle Griet in Ghent it is (or was) served in a particularly special glass, a shorter version of the 'yard of ale'. Since this type of glass has a round bottom and no visible means of support (sounds familiar, doesn't it?) it is supplied with a wooden stand to hold it upright. This is an expensive combination and the landlord got tired of people souveniring the whole thing. His answer was to take a deposit on it in the form of one of the drinker's shoes. This was placed in a basket and hoisted to the ceiling by a pulley, only to be returned when the glass and stand came back!

Another cafe in Ghent, De Hopduvel, has a specialty beer brewed for it by the Slaghmuylder brewery, under the name of Stropken. This is a not only a beautiful beer but the name is a bi-lingual pun. It comes from a historical event in the Middle Ages when the burghers of Ghent got a little too uppity for the Holy Roman Emperor, Charles V. He had them rounded up and, to demonstrate his power of life and death over them, paraded them around the streets with nooses round their necks. Ever since then the people of Ghent have borne the nickname *Stropken*, which means 'little rope' or 'noose'. The pun comes from the name of the proprietor of De Hopduvel who first devised the beer, and the label, Antoine Denooze.

One of the strongest beers in the world is brewed under the name Bush Beer by the Dubuisson family in Hainaut. Bush Beer is a very thick, mouth-filling, strongly malty brew, which is hardly surprising considering it is bottled at a strength of 12% alc/vol (9.5% alc/wt)! Finally, as if to confirm the to German-style traditionalists may already supect—that the whole Belgian beer scene is crazy—one highly successful brewery makes a whole range of beers under their company title De Dolle Brouwers, 'The Mad Brewers'.

Flanders brown ale

This is a peculiarly Belgian style of dark ale that is related to the British style only by its colour; everything else about it is different. The best known example of Flanders brown is Liefmann's Goudenband, which used to be brewed in a small and very traditional brewery near Oudenarde in West Flanders until the operation and the name were taken over by the Riva brewery in nearby Dentergem. It seems that some of the traditions have gone by the board now, simply because the new owners felt they could make exactly the same beer by more streamlined methods—and with much better equipment. In the old days, the wort used to be boiled for something like eight hours; now it's back around the normal figure of one to two hours. As it turned out, the reason for the long boil was simply that the old kettle took hours to get up to speed! At Oudenarde, the hot wort used to be transferred to a long shallow coolship where it was left for a few hours with the deliberate aim of picking up some of the local wild yeasts. When cool it was then transferred to wooden barrels where it would pick up some further residual yeast, then was pitched with the main yeast.

The combination of these three yeasts produced a beer with a distinctly tart flavour, not as sour as some Belgian specialties but still definitely fruity and acidic. The beer was then conditioned at normal temperatures for six weeks before being blended with another batch that had been maturing for some months; the resulting blend was bottled with priming sugars and more yeast and left to condition for three

FIGURE 7.1

*Udo Stork, brewmaster
at King of Flanders
brewpub, Augsburg*

LAURIE STRACHAN

FIGURE 7.2

*Old wooden
fermenters, Bamberg
Brewery Museum*

LAURIE STRACHAN

months before being released. As a special touch each bottle was wrapped in tissue paper. To add to all this, it was (and is) possible to buy the beer in special large bottles up to the size of champagne-style jeroboams (20 bottles' worth) for special occasions. Nowadays most of this process still goes on; the difference is that mashing and boiling are carried out at Dentergem and the wort then trucked to Oudenarde for fermentation. Being already tart and fruity, Goudenband makes an ideal base for a fruit beer and Liefmann's macerate cherries in some batches to produce a non-lambic kriek.

A style closely associated with Flanders brown, and in fact considered by some to be a sub-genre of the style, takes this tartness a stage further, to the point of being actually sour. The classic of this style is Rodenbach, also from West Flanders, which gets its tartness partly from storage in untreated wooden tuns and partly from the yeast used. The majority of the beer is blended with a proportion of aged beer to give a slightly less aggressive tartness while the aged beer itself is also bottled under the label Grand Cru. The lactic fermentation which results gives this average-strength (4.5–5% alc/vol, 3.5–4% alc/wt) beer a very individual flavour, the kind of flavour that would draw gasps of horror from pilsener brewers to whom cleanliness is not just next to godliness but *is* godliness. It also makes it a difficult beer to enjoy at first taste, particularly if you have not been warned. Once acquired though, the taste is unforgettable and many Belgians consider Rodenbach one of their great classics. Others like Zulte have tried to copy it but without achieving quite the same success in balancing the flavours—and in a beer like this with such strongly acidic overtones, balance is not just important but critical.

Saisons

As with many other traditional brewing areas, Belgium has its seasonal beers; in particular, many of the small breweries produce special strong, dark, sweet ales for Christmas. But there is another style, saisons, which is neither dark nor particularly strong, which originated as a seasonal beer for the summer but is now drunk all year round. Saisons are almost the *bières ordinaires* of the Belgian beer world for, unlike most of the other Belgian ale styles, they are not extravagantly flavoured nor are they particularly strong. Of course, strength here is a relative concept. A Belgian specialty beer cafe owner once told me he had cut down severely on his drinking of strong beers and now was restricting himself to a limit of 6% alc/vol (5% alc/wt). He could drink those all night! However, saisons are not entirely conventional in makeup; some use honey in the kettle, one is spiced with ginger. Once again. it's all relative. As their name implies, saisons come from the French-speaking part of Belgium, often known as Wallonia, where, although they do not boast quite so many breweries, they are not far behind in consumption and certainly not at all backward in brewing skills. Classics of the style are Saison de Silly (no reference to Monty Python intended), brewed in a farmhouse in the village of the same name, and Saison 1900, named after an important year in the history of the Lefevbre brewery.

German ales

Kölsch

Ales were brewed in Germany for many centuries before the idea of lagering became widespread and they are still popular in many parts of the country. Their stronghold, however, is in the Rhineland. There Cologne (Köln) swears by its very special beer, kölsch, while its neighbour city and deadly rival, Düsseldorf, specialises in another and very different top-fermenter, altbier.

Kölsch is not the only beer in the world which has its own *appellation controlée* but it must be the most tightly controlled of all beer styles. The Kölsch Convention limits the use of the name Kölsch to breweries within 50 kilometres of Köln Cathedral—although one or two exceptions are made for breweries just outside the area that had traditionally been brewing kölsch for many years before the Convention was formed.

The beer itself is almost a hybrid of ale and lager techniques, although the use of a top-fermenting yeast puts it squarely in the ale camp. It is almost as pale as a pilsener, it has about the same alcohol level (5% alc/vol, 6% alc/wt) and its flavour profile shows some similarities, such as a light but distinct sulphury tinge, particularly noticeable when the beer is not chilled. Brewing techniques do not appear to be actually specified by the Convention and they vary from brewery to brewery. Some do an infusion mash, others stick to the old decoction

FIGURE 8.1
*Sünner Brewery,
Cologne (Köln)*
LAURIE STRACHAN

FIGURE 8.2
*Brewery dray,
Cologne (Köln)*
LAURIE STRACHAN

technique. At one of the bigger (and ever-expanding) kölsch breweries, P. J. Früh's Cölner Hofbräu, an infusion mash using only spring barley is followed by a one-hour boil with noble German hops such as Hallertauer and Tettnang. Both of these steps are taken in order not to darken the brew or to lessen the formation of a head, which might be jeopardised by the top-fermentation. After an initial fermentation of up to a week, most of the yeast is removed. This used to be done by transferring to a second tank but at Früh they use just one tank and remove the yeast either by drawing it off the bottom of conical fermenters or by skimming it off the top, depending on the flocculation characteristics of the particular yeast used. The beer is then lagered at around 0°C (32°F) for a month before packaging.

Something like 70 per cent of kölsch is served on draught and there is another city tradition of selling it in small barrels called *Pittermänschen* of 5, 10, 15, 20 and 30 gallons. They are named after St Peter the Martyr who is the patron saint of the Köln brewers and whose gory end is celebrated as part of a huge stained-glass window in the cathedral. These barrels used to be made of wood, and wooden ones can still be obtained, but polythene-lined steel is now more common for reasons of convenience.

Kölsch also has its own very strict traditions in the way it is served and consumed, although they are shared to a large extent by neighbouring Düsseldorf and its altbier brewers and consumers. In fact, the ales of Köln and Düsseldorf are not just beers—they are a complete serving and consuming system. The way they are served makes it difficult, though not impossible, to get drunk and that in turn means the brewer can sell an almost infinite amount of beer. Turnover in the big *Brauhausen* and *Ausshanken* like Früh, Päffgen and Küppers are incredibly high. It's also a system that depends very much on peoples' innate honesty—the hardest part of drinking in a Köln *Brauhaus* is finding someone to pay.

Here's how it works at P. J. Früh's pub in Am Hof close to the cathedral (though of course everything in central Köln is close to the cathedral). The *Brauerei* used to be a working brewery but demand became too big for it to handle so in 1986 the brewery was relocated to the industrial area in the city's north. This produced a double advantage—much higher output and more space in which to serve customers in the city. Since a dedicated kölsch house like this sells only one beer—its own if it is a *Hausbrauerei* or, if not, the product of one of the big, or biggish, Kölsch breweries—this means the glasses are all the same shape and size, the traditional (in fact, mandatory, under the Kölsch Convention) narrow 200 ml cylinder.

One functionary stands by a huge wooden barrel doing nothing but filling glasses at an incredibly rapid rate. Presumably because he is experienced at this he knows exactly how far to fill the glass so that when the foam subsides it will come to within about two fingers of the top. Kölsch is a highly effervescent beer though it is not kegged or casked under high pressure; the natural conditioning of the beer gives it a substantial head without making it gassy—another reason why it is so easy to drink. The measure looks a little rough and ready but presumably it averages out over the night and nobody seems to complain about being short-served. When the barrel runs out, the pourer pushes it to one side and pulls up another barrel from a kind of dumb waiter at his side. Once that is in position, he slides the old barrel onto the dumb waiter and dispatches it down to the cellar.

The *Köbes* come to the serving area and fill their deep circular trays with glasses at an equally mind-boggling speed then race off to place the glasses in front of the customers. The assumption is simple—if the customer has an empty glass in front of them, or no glass at all, they want a beer. If they don't want a beer, they pay and go. A tally of how much each customer ordered is kept on their coaster. Since there is only one beer at one price, the arithmetic at the end is simple. The *Köbes* wear a standard uniform of dark slacks and a blue shirt, supplemented by a blue sweater or cardigan in the colder months, and usually have a leather pouch like a sporran hanging at their waists to handle cash and change. You never set eyes on a cash register let alone a computer.

It is surely the most efficient way of serving beer ever devised, with benefits for both customer and brewer, and it works particularly well simply because everything is standardised under the Kölsch Convention. I saw one pub in the Altstadt, the Old Town—close to the Rhine where there is a great variety of pubs and restaurants—offering a 'metre of kölsch' which apparently meant a row of the glasses which, side by side, measured a metre. Whether there was a bulk discount I don't know.

The *Köbes* have a tradition of being aggressive and even insolent to customers, something which the drinkers of Köln obviously enjoy but which clearly distresses the townsfolk who have to sell the place to tourists and are afraid this kind of cheerful effrontery will be misunderstood and will do no good for the city's image as a friendly place. Perhaps they are being just a little too cautious. Perhaps it also goes some way to explaining why experiments with the recruitment of women waiters have not been particularly successful; it seems the traditional

customers just don't like the idea. It's one thing being insulted by a man, but from a woman it might be taken as a slight on your manhood.

A typical story told of a *Köbes* goes like this. A customer asks for water instead of a glass of kölsch. The waiter sneers: 'You have your own soap and towel, I suppose.'

Another story is of a customer asking for a pils in a kölsch house. The waiter pretends to look out the door at the pub across the road and says: 'They're closing soon but if you hurry, you'll get one.'

That's Köln and kölsch—a beer culture not to be missed.

Altbier

Düsseldorf is no more than a couple of hours drive from Köln and the beer cultures in the two cities have some strong similarities, including the manner of serving and the ubiquitous *Köbes*, yet the two cities have a long-standing rivalry, not unlike Liverpool and Manchester, Glasgow and Edinburgh, Sydney and Melbourne. Naturally, each swears by its own beer. Both beers are made by the old top-fermenting methods by which all beer was brewed before the Bavarians happened on bottom-fermentation and lagering. But they are quite different products. Whereas kölsch is pale golden like a lager and shines in the glass, Düsseldorf's altbier looks, and to some extent tastes, like a British-style ale, dark, chocolatey brown, clear but hardly sparkling. It too rates at around 5% alc/vol (4% alc/wt).

Altbier is a generic style that can be found in many parts of Germany but Düsseldorf is the only city in which it is the staple, in fact dominant, beer style. *Alt* means simply 'old' and refers to the fact that this is a beer brewed in the old top-fermenting style. Altbiers can be made with pale base malts to which are added roasted malts to achieve the colour or they can be brewed entirely with an amber malt like Munich malt, as is the case at the Schumacher brewery in

FIGURE 8.4

Herr Enderman,

brewmaster at

Schumacher brewery,

Düsseldorf, Germany

LAURIE STRACHAN

the heart of Düsseldorf's shopping and business centre. Schumacher's alt is brewed with a combination of infusion and decoction mashes in a brewery that is a combination of ancient and modern, as is so often the case with mid-sized German breweries. Cooling is still by coolship in combination with an exterior flow cooler, and measurements are still taken with big glass hydrometers, although many other brewery functions are controlled by computer.

Düsseldorf also boasts one of Germany's most famous brewpubs, Zum Uerige, in the Altstadt close to the Rhine, a cheerful, hail-fellow-well-met tavern where customers jostle together in front of the shiny copper of the brewing kettle just off one of the main drinking halls. Uerige's alt is probably the most bitter of the several examples of the style available in Düsseldorf, the flavour dominated by roasted malts and bitter hops. The product of the other big pub brewery, Zum Schlüssel, part of the Gatzweiler group, is balanced more to the middle palate with some fruity sweetness, although the characteristic alt bitterness is still there at the end. Schumacher's product is dominated by the flavour of the single malt (no, nothing to do with Scotch whisky) used in its production, a Munich-style tailored for its own needs. The result takes a little getting used to. Perhaps the best balanced of all comes from another pub brewery, Im Füchsen, also in the Altstadt, the rather touristy old town of Düsseldorf which the tourism people have dubbed 'the longest bar in the world'.

FIGURE 8.5

Coolship at Schumacher brewery, Düsseldorf,

Germany

LAURIE STRACHAN

FIGURE 8.6

Tram advertising Gatzweiler Altbier, Düsseldorf,

Germany

LAURIE STRACHAN

Other ales

American ales

Ales virtually died out in the United States, with Prohibition finishing off what the lager revolution started, but in recent years there has been a major revival of the style, mainly by micro-brewers of various kinds. The most interesting is the US interpretation of pale ale, which leans towards a greater use of aroma hops than the English original and can be quite floral in the nose; while the most popular commercial variant of the style is cream ale which is a light-bodied and usually pale ale (though sometimes bottom-fermented) with a relatively bland character. The classic example of the US pale ale style is the pale ale produced at the Sierra Nevada brewery in California.

Australian ales

Although Australian brewing has long been dominated by lagers, ales have retained a tiny foothold. The two New South Wales breweries Tooths (now part of Carlton United Breweries) and Tooheys both have olds which they say are top-fermented in the old style. But really, the most interesting ale in Australia is Cooper's Sparkling Ale. This is a beer produced by traditional methods of open fermentation in wooden vats at ambient temperature; it is then bottle-conditioned, or in the case of the keg product, keg-conditioned in metal kegs.

Cooper's great achievement is to have succeeded in brewing a traditional ale at ambient temperatures in a climate which would seem to be totally unsuited to it. The secret obviously lies in their yeast, which has a wide range of temperature tolerance, and this makes it not only an interesting beer to drink, but a wonderful one from which to culture a yeast for home brewing purposes. Many other Australian beers call themselves ales but are clearly not, under the definition we are using. Good examples are Castlemaine Bitter Ale and Cascade Pale Ale which, while undoubtedly successful products, are nothing but lagers under a different name.

The great beer styles: wheat beers

Although the great majority of beers are made from malted barley, there is a whole sub-genre of beers that also use a proportion of malted wheat, or even raw wheat, in the mash, and this, often in combination with special yeasts, gives them a quite different flavour from malt-based beers. The proportion of wheat used varies greatly from beer to beer and from place to place, but the usual mix is around half-and-half, barley and wheat. These days wheat beers are found all over the world but the historic centres of wheat beer production are Germany and Belgium.

10 German wheat beers

German wheat beers differ most obviously from their Belgian equivalents in that they are subject, like all German beers, to the purity law, the *Reinheitsgebot*, which prevents brewers from using anything but malt, hops, yeast and water to produce beer. Thus German wheat beers universally use malted wheat in the mash, whereas in Belgium it is not unusual to find as much as 40 per cent raw, unmalted wheat in the mix.

Germany has historically produced two quite different styles of wheat beer in two widely separated areas. The region of Berlin in the east of the country is the home of a quite unique specialty, Berliner weisse. *Weisse* is simply German for 'white' and, not surprisingly, the beer gets its name because not only it is very pale but it is also unfiltered and the tiny protein and yeast particles floating in the beer give it a cloudy appearance that could be taken as almost white. Berliner weisse is predominantly a summer drink. It is low in alcohol (3% alc/vol, 2.5% alc/wt) and has a tart, lightly acid finish that comes from the element of lactic fermentation in the special yeast used. As a result it is one of the few beers that can actually benefit from the addition of a sweeter element in the glass and it is the custom in Berlin to add a dash of raspberry syrup or essence of the herb woodruff, according to the drinker's taste, to the big round goblet in which the beer is served.

FIGURE 10.1
Bavarian weizen
(weissbier)
FRANZISKANER, MUNICH,
GERMANY

Berliner weisse is found all over Germany these days, as is the other great German wheat style, Bavarian weizen—*Weizen* from the German for 'wheat'. The problem that now arises is that in Bavaria a weizen is often referred to as a weissbier so you have to be sure what you are asking for. In practice, if you are in the south you are almost certain to be served a weizen if you ask for a weissbier. Weizen is traditionally served unfiltered but a filtered version is available nowadays under the designation 'kristall'. But beware, it seems to have become trendy in some places to add a slice of lemon to a kristall, after the fashion of Corona and its slice of lime in the United States. The idea is nonsense as the lemon simply destroys the subtle malt and yeast flavours that are still evident even in the filtered version.

The real, unfiltered weizen is an absolute riot of flavours. The yeasts used in combination with the wheat malt produce a bizarre (by comparison with standard malt beers) phenolic flavour that is like a sour/sweet, spicy fruitiness. It is often compared with the flavour of rich pears or even peaches and apricots—and this is probably one of the few cases where this kind of over-the-top comparison, so beloved of wine writers, is properly applicable to beer. To those used to the malt/hops balance of 'normal' beers, this phenolic flavour can come as quite a shock and be difficult to enjoy; the aroma and the flavour on the front palate make you instantly suspect there is something wrong. However, once you get used to it, this particular characteristic becomes almost addictive and definitely an essential part of the pleasurable experience of drinking a Weizen. There is something deeply satisfying about seeing a Weizen in its distinctive, tall, flaring 700 ml glass, with the top third accommodating the huge fluffy head, set down in front of you—and drinking it is a taste adventure in itself.

Flavours vary quite substantially from brew to brew with the biggest differences being in the degree of phenolic flavour imparted by the particular yeast. In the huge beer hall of the Hofbräuhaus in Munich you will find a weizen that is only mildly accented with fruit and spice, whereas in the nearby Augustiner Restaurant the weizen is a more pungent and characterful brew. The Erdinger brewery just outside Munich sells its nicely balanced weizen all over Germany. Like Berliner weisse, weizen has expanded out of its historical heartland and can be found all over the country, although Bavaria remains the area with much the greatest variety.

The great majority of weizens are pale beers but there is a parallel dark style, dunkelweizen. This is about the same dark, chocolatey shade as a dunkel lager and like that style is dominated by the flavour of the dark malts, reducing the impact of the yeast phenolics to no more than an accent. Dunkelweizens are found all over Bavaria but are less popular outside that great brewing state.

Although these styles originated in Germany they can now be found in many other parts of the world. Micro-breweries in the US often offer a weizen as part of their range and one of Australia's major brewers, the Foster's Brewing Group, now has a wheat beer, Redback, in its stable as the result of taking over the Matilda Bay micro-brewery in Perth, Western Australia. Redback is loosely modelled on the Bavarian kristall weizen style in that it is pale and filtered and yields some phenolic flavours (though much less than it used to before the takeover).

11 Belgian wheat beers

Although Germany is much the biggest producer and consumer of wheat beers, the wheat beers of Belgium are even more interesting. There are basically two streams of wheat beer production in Belgium—wit or 'white' beers, not dissimilar to some of the German styles, and lambic beers, which are like no other beers on earth and, in effect, represent the survival of a technique of beer making that died out in other places centuries ago.

Wit beer

Production of wheat beers used to be commonplace in those areas of Belgium where wheat was the staple grain but over the years it fell away, dying out in the years after World War II as standardised lagers took over more and more of the market, and it was gradually assumed that such odd specialties were things of the past. However, the tradition never quite vanished and in the '60s it was revived with enormous success.

Wit beers are a distinct style of their own but, like most things connected with Belgian brewing, that style is subject to some very individual interpretations. Some have hints of phenolics, some show lactic notes, some are flavoured with oddities like coriander and curaçao, others mash from a mixture that includes not just malted barley and raw wheat but some oats as well. They tend not to be particularly highly hopped, of about average strength (4–5% alc/vol, 3–4% alc/wt) and like German wheats are often cloudy, partly because of the amount of proteins yielded by the raw grains and partly because they are bottle-conditioned and thus have a fair amount of yeast in suspension. Like Berliner weisse, the name 'wit' comes from this cloudy appearance.

The classic Belgian wit, and the beer that revived the style, is Hoegaarden, brewed by the De Kluis brewery in the village of the same name in the east of Brabant. The area was historically famous for its wheat beers and De Kluis simply turned the clock back. Hoegaarden is a sweetish but well-balanced beer with rich flavours from the mixture of ingredients used in its brewing. It has some subdued phenolic elements and a definite fruitiness without quite delivering the pungency of a Bavarian weizen. Another good example of the style, again sweetly fruity but with a clean finish is Blanche de Bruges, produced in the historic city of the same name.

Lambic beers

The specialty beers of Belgium are some of the most diverse and fascinating in the world, yet when compared with lambic beers they actually begin to seem quite conservative. Lambic beers are a throwback to the ancient world, the age of Sumer. Knowing nothing about yeast, not even suspecting its existence, these earliest known brewers used to mash bread into warm water and simply wait for something to happen. Fortunately for the future of beer, things did happen as first the warm water leached the sugars out of the bread then wild yeasts and bacteria started to feed on the result. The result was the first beer. Today in Belgium, and more particularly in the Payottenland area of the Senne Valley near Brussels, there are brewers who do much the same sort of thing and produce a whole range of beautiful and characterful beers.

Lambic brewers don't mash bread into water, they mash grains, like everybody else in the modern brewing world, but from then on their processes are a direct link to ancient practices. They put together a mash of approximately 60 per cent barley malt and 40 per cent wheat, either malted or unmalted (the proportions vary slightly from brewer to brewer), sparge it then boil it with hops, more or less as usual. The difference starts from here on in for they do not use fresh hops as virtually everyone else does, but hops that are at least three years old. The reason is that they are not looking for bitterness in this beer, they want only the flavour, aroma and preserving qualities of the hops.

However, it is the next step in the process that sets lambic beers apart from the rest. The wort is cooled by running it into long, flat coolships. It is then left there for 12 hours or more with all the windows, skylights, everything, open to the outdoors—for this is where lambics get their yeast, from nature. True lambics are the only beers in the world brewed by spontaneous fermentation, using only wild yeasts; no other yeasts are pitched. After cooling, the wort is transferred to wooden tuns where it picks up further yeasts and bacteria resident in the wood and in its tiny cracks and crevices. So begins a long and complex fermentation process directed by nature itself. The wort goes through yeast, bacterial and lactic fermentations over a period of around eight months. After this the newly fermented beer is blended with beer at least a year older and the resulting mix is bottled and given a secondary fermentation in the bottle which, ideally, should last for another year. The beer thus produced is known as 'gueuze' and this is the basic style of lambic beer.

After this highly unusual production process it's no surprise that gueuze doesn't taste much like any other beer. In fact, if you were to be given it without being told what it was you might well pick it as some sort of derivative of champagne or other sparkling wine. In colour it is a pale, golden brown, slightly hazy because unfiltered; it is highly effervescent thanks to the secondary fermentation in the bottle; and it gives off a subtle mix of aromas in which the yeasts are the most obvious. The flavours are complex, slightly sweet, fruity, lightly malty with a hint of hops and a touch of sherry mixed with other subtle compounds. Truly an amazing beer.

But that's not where the lambic world ends. In fact, for another whole series of beers, it's only the beginning. Keeping alive yet another old brewing tradition, the lambic brewers use their product as the base for beers flavoured with fruit. There seem to be two explanations for this, both based on historical necessity. In the first place, before hops came into prominence and eventually dominated the brewing world, beers were flavoured with all sorts of mixtures. Most prominent was the herbal mixture gruit, but where that was not readily available and fresh stone fruit was plentiful, they might well have used that. The second explanation is that this lambic would not always have been stable in the summer months after it had stopped fermenting. So, innkeepers and publicans might well have added fruit like cherries and raspberries to the beer they had stored in order to start a second fermentation and keep the beer alive and fresh.

Whatever the reason, the practice of putting fruit into lambic beer is an old one and one still practised in Belgium. After this addition and the subsequent re-fermentation, the beer is renamed according to the fruit used. So the cherry beer is called 'kriek', the Flemish word for cherries, and the raspberry beer 'framboise' after the French word for raspberries. No, it isn't consistent but that's what you get in a determinedly bilingual country like Belgium.

There is one other lambic specialty that used to be particularly popular in Belgium but is not so widespread now, though it can still be found in the beer cafes of Brussels—faro. This is a young and very tart lambic to which is added a little candi sugar for sweetening to make an enjoyably drinkable and refreshing beer that still boasts more complexity than most conventional beers could dream of.

Nearly all the famous lambic breweries are to be found in the Payottenland. Perhaps the best known is Cantillon in Anderlecht, which is not only an active brewery but also a lambic museum open to the public. Its Grand Cru and Framboise are both classics. Timmerman's at Itterbeek brews a most delicious kriek, soft, fruity and refreshing, an ideal aperitif; while Lindeman's, set in a small farmhouse, exports its Faro, Gueuze, Kriek and Framboise all over the world. In the Brussels cafe Mort Subite (Sudden Death) you will find lambics brewed for the house by the brewery in nearby Kobbegem. Incidentally the name has nothing to do with the potential risks of drinking the beer; it's the name of a dice game played in the cafe. Mort Subite and the beautifully decorated La Becasse, both quite close to the Grand Place at the heart of Brussels, are essential stops for anyone interested in Belgian beer in general and lambic in particular.

Brewing the great beers: ingredients and methods

Beers vary greatly in colour and flavour throughout the world, from the pale yellow of a pilsener to the black of a stout. The differences come mainly from the use of different grains, yeasts and hops.

12 Ingredients

Grains

Base malts

Malted grains are the basis of virtually all beer and they fall into two basic categories, those that are used in bulk and those used in small quantities. The latter are often called specialty malts, because they are usually malted grains that have been given special treatment, usually by roasting, to give them a darker colour and a richer, caramelised or, in some cases, even charcoal flavour.

A typical beer, whatever its style or colour, will be made mainly from a base malt, a standard, lightly kilned malt, to which other specialty malts are added in various quantities depending on the style and colour desired. Base malts are generally the palest of the malt family but they do vary from country to country. For instance, British pale ale malts are generally darker than European or American lager malts. However, it is possible to brew all but the very palest of lagers using pale ale malts while lager malts can be used to brew the darkest beers.

Malted barley is a little like coffee beans but more so. Coffee beans come in different degrees of colour, from a light brown to the darkest espresso. The different degrees of roasting give different levels of caramelisation and result in different flavours in the finished cup of coffee.

Malts come in a much wider range of colours, from the pale gold of base malts to the almost charcoal darkness of the highly roasted specialties. Naturally they will give quite different colours and flavours to the finished beer. The degree of colour of malts and the beers that are made from them is rated by three different scales. Lovibond (L) and Standard Reference Method (SRM) are close enough to each other to be considered identical, while the European Brewing Convention (EBC) scale differs considerably. For ease and consistency the Lovibond scale will be used here. Base malts will usually be rated at around 2L for lager malts and 3–4L for pale ale malts.

There are further differences among base malts that arise from the basic differences between different varieties of barley, from the climate in which they are grown and from the way in which they are treated during malting. These variables result in different levels of protein and starch in the malted grain and can determine the way in which they must be mashed to extract the sugars. Malts with high protein levels need to be mashed in at lower temperatures to ensure these proteins are converted into starches before they are further changed into fermentable sugars. Malts with low protein levels need only be mashed in one step at the saccharification temperature.

Fortunately home brewers almost everywhere have access to low-protein malts and it is strongly recommended that these malts be used wherever possible. The business of brewing from grains is lengthy enough without adding any extra work.

Specialty malts

It is quite possible to brew beautiful beers without using anything but base malts but you will only be able to brew beers of one colour—pale gold. If you wish to try your hand at any other style you will have to use specialty malts. The way these are used depends very much on the style of malt.

VIENNA MALT   A European malt kilned to about 4L, used to make the classic amber vienna and oktoberfest styles. Because this is still a very pale malt, it can be used in quite large quantities to give a beer an amber colour and a more malty flavour. However, it is usually harder to find than pale malt and more expensive—and much the same effect can be obtained by using pale malt and adding a small portion of a darker specialty malt such as crystal malt.

MUNICH MALT   Another European malt, kilned to around 5–6L, which can be used as a base malt but is better as only part of a mash as it can impart a harsh, tannic quality to a beer if it is not balanced and treated absolutely correctly. Again, this may be hard to obtain in some places so ordinary pale malt can be used with an addition of a darker specialty.

CRYSTAL MALT   This is the most important, useful and widespread of the specialty malts. Crystal malt is more than simply a highly roasted pale malt. At the stage in production when pale malt would be dried, for crystal malt the temperature is raised and the wet, germinated barley is virtually mashed inside its own kernel, which becomes crystallised or caramelised (in Europe it's known as caramel malt). The malt finishes up a reddish-brown colour with a nice-

ly toffee-ish flavour. Colour can vary from 20L to 120L and it should come labelled accordingly. Because it has undergone this internal mashing process, crystal malt does not have to be mashed to extract the sugars from it—simply soaking in hot water will release them. This makes it an ideal ingredient for use in malt extract recipes. In all-grain recipes, however, crystal malt is always added to the mash, simply for convenience.

CHOCOLATE MALT   Malted barley roasted in a kiln to a dark brown colour, around 400L. Chocolate malt is useful in very small quantities to give a caramel edge to pale ales, and other malty beers, in larger amounts to produce dark beers like porters, milds and stouts. Like the other very dark malts, chocolate malt yields no sugars to the wort; therefore it can be added without increasing the strength of the beer.

ROAST MALT/BLACK PATENT MALT Malted barley roasted to 500L in a kiln till it turns a very dark brown, almost black. Roast malt is used as a colouring and flavouring agent in beer in even smaller quantities than crystal or chocolate malt. Used sparingly it can help give an edge of almost charcoal bitterness to a bitter or a Scottish-style ale. It is used in larger quantities in stouts, porters and doppelbocks where the resulting beer is intended to be very dark, sometimes almost opaque.

ROAST BARLEY   Unlike the other specialty grains, roast barley is not made from malted barley. In this case ordinary dried barley is used and it is roasted to 400L. The result is a flavour with subtle differences from the roasted malts, though the colouring effect is similar. Like the other dark malts, it can also be used in very small quantities to flavour paler beers but perhaps its most famous use is to help give the dark colour and dry palate to Guinness stout.

WHEAT MALT   Wheat malt is wheat grain that has been malted in the same way as barley malt but it has its own properties and imparts its own unique characteristics to a beer. Wheat malt has a higher protein content than barley malt and proteins tend to leave hazes in beer, which is one reason many wheat beers, such as Berliner weisse, are left deliberately cloudy. It can also leave a mildly phenolic or clovey flavour in the beer, a noticeable feature of the wheat beers of Bavaria. If wheat makes up a significant proportion of a beer's grain bill, say 30 per cent or more, it becomes designated as a wheat beer. However, wheat malt can also be used as an adjunct in otherwise all-barley beers. It is often included in the makeup of beers like some English bitters because its high protein content helps create and maintain the head and at the same time accentuates the beer's malty accent.

Adjuncts

Adjuncts are simply materials other than malted barley which are used by brewers for a variety of reasons, whether to save money, to aid clarity, or to give a certain character. Some of these adjuncts have to be mashed and even, in their basic forms, have to be cooked first. To save yourself this trouble you can buy them in the form of flakes, which are available in health food stores. These flakes are grains which have been crushed through rollers at high pressure; the resultant heat gelatinises them and makes them ready for mashing without further cooking.

These adjuncts can be useful in small quantities either to give the beer a particular character or to improve aspects of its appearance or flavour.

Grain adjuncts

Brewers sometimes use unmalted grains for the particular effects they have on a beer's composition and also because they are cheaper than malt. Unmalted barley is often used in smallish quantities because the unmodified proteins in the grain give better head retention. At the same time though, unmalted adjuncts can cause haze problems. These can be solved by allowing the finished beer longer to clear or by more thorough filtering.

The other important factor about the use of unmalted grains is that they cannot be mashed as they are; they must be cooked first to gelatinise their starches before the mash enzymes can convert them to sugars. There is a way around this, however. Health food shops sell grains in the form of flakes, essentially the same thing as corn flakes but without any added flavourings. These flakes have been manufactured by running whole grains between powerful rollers. The pressure of the rollers creates high heat that gelatinises the starches in the grain. As a result, these grain flakes can be added straight to the mash. As far as home brewers are concerned, this saves another step in the process and has much to recommend it. In recipes in this book which call for unmalted adjuncts they will always be listed as flakes.

There are five principal unmalted grain adjuncts.

BARLEY   Used to give body and a grainy character to the beer as well as to aid in head retention. Helps give Guinness its famous head and is used in a number of well-known British beers for the same purpose, as well as to give body and a mildly grainy flavour which, in moderation, can add to the beer's complexity.

RICE   Gives a lightness to both body and flavour without the 'cidery' effect of cane sugar. Rice is an important part of the formulation of the world's biggest selling beer, Budweiser.

MAIZE   Used extensively in the United States (where it is particularly cheap) and to some extent in Britain. It adds a corny flavour that is easily recognisable when you know what to look for.

UNMALTED WHEAT   This can be used in the mash but only in small quantities as it contains no enzymes. If you wish to make a typical wheat beer of half-and-half barley malt and wheat malt, you must use malted wheat.

OATS   Used in oatmeal stout, hence the name.

Non-grain adjuncts

There is scarcely any limit to what can be put into beer—one historic recipe, Cock Ale, actually called for the inclusion of a whole chicken in the brew. In practice though, non-grain adjuncts can be divided into those used to give lightness of body and flavour and those used to impart a special flavour.

Sugars

Rather than adding corn or rice to the mash, brewers may opt to include extra sugars later in the process to achieve much the same effect with less effort.

CANE SUGAR (SUCROSE)   ·Presumably because Britain once had a thriving trade with its sugar-cane growing colonies in the West Indies, and sugar was therefore cheap and plentiful, British brewers have traditionally used cane sugar to dilute the protein content of their beers and keep down haze problems, which might otherwise have been a major drawback in traditional, unfiltered real ales. As a result, British brew-

ers have become experts in the judicious use of this adjunct and many of their finest beers contain cane sugar products. The important word here is 'judicious'; the instruction by most home brew kit manufacturers to add 1 kg (2 lb) of sugar to a can kit should be takes with a grain of salt, so to speak. Cane sugar should be used very sparingly in home brewing otherwise the resulting beers will tend to have a sour, cidery flavour and aroma. Again, this is a characteristic that is all too easy to detect.

CORN SUGAR (DEXTROSE)   Widely used in North America and less extensively in other areas. The effects on body and flavour are similar to the use of corn in the mash but adding it in sugar form means it can go straight into the kettle at the boiling stage. Dextrose can be added in larger quantities than sucrose without the beer developing a cidery effect but should still be used with caution.

HONEY   Honey is a mix of the two sugars fructose and sucrose plus various other herbal flavourings. It is highly fermentable and will lighten the body of a beer but it should be used sparingly because it will impart very strong flavours. Those who have used honey extensively warn that only light honeys should be used in brewing.

MOLASSES (SUCROSE)   A by-product of sugar-refining, molasses (also known as treacle) has a pungent and easily recognised flavour which will tend to dominate the palate of a beer unless used in tiny amounts. At best, it can give an interestingly caramel edge.

Hops

Although many things have been, and still are, used to enhance the flavour of beer, nothing has ever achieved the near-universality of hops. Hops and beer are now so closely intertwined in the popular mind that it is not uncommon to find beer drinkers who believe it is hops rather

FIGURE 12.1
Hop farming
THE HOP ATLAS 1994, P. 24, JOH. BARTH & SOHN, NUREMBERG

century, it took several hundred years before their use became widespread even in this area. It was not until the fourteenth century that the use of hops spread as far as Holland and Belgium and from there to Britain.

Hops were initially used as a preservative as much as a flavouring for in those times, and in fact until the advent of refrigeration, it was difficult to keep beer, or anything else organic, for any length of time without it spoiling. It was found that the hop oils and resins acted as a kind of natural disinfectant, inhibiting bacterial and wild yeast infections. (Interestingly enough, this aspect of hop chemistry is once again being researched and revived by the big hop merchants as the world seeks ever new weapons against bacteria and the merchants seek new markets in

FIGURE 12.2
Humulus lupus—*the true hop*
ETCHING 1796, THE HOP ATLAS 1994, P. 25, JOH. BARTH & SOHN, NUREMBERG

than malted grains which are the principal ingredient in beer. We do not know for certain when brewers started using hops to flavour and preserve their beer. Little solid evidence has been unearthed to indicate even where hops came from and whether they are native to Europe (where their cultivation began) or were an introduced species. Although hops grow wild in parts of Europe, it is not known whether they are the precursors of cultivated hops or simply represent the descendants of plants that, as it were, escaped from captivity. Archaeological finds that prove beer was brewed in Germany as far back as the eighth century AD have produced no evidence to indicate hops were involved. What is known is that well into the second millennium many brewers were still flavouring their beer with the mixture of wild herbs known as gruit. However, historians believe that while the use of hops by some brewers in southern Germany had begun as early as the seventh a time of diminishing use of their products in beer.) Nowadays the chief purpose of using hops in beer is to give bitterness to what would otherwise be a sweet and quite sickly liquid. Attempts to bitter beer by adding the chemical constituents of hops have not succeeded, probably because the whole hops also yield important flavours which go to make up the character of beer—and different hops give different bitterness and flavour characteristics.

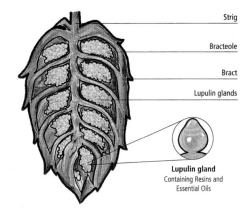

FIGURE 12.3

Cross-section of a hop cone

HOP VARIETIES EUROPEAN GROWN 1994, JOH. BARTH & SOHN, NUREMBERG

Hops are the flowers of a plant that goes by the botanical name of *Humulus lupulus*, a member of the hemp family, or Cannabinaceae. Hops are related to the elm, mulberry and nettle and grow best in cool temperate climates. As a result most of the world's big hop-growing areas are situated in zones between 35 and 55° latitude north and south of the equator. The fact that they largely coincide with the great barley-growing regions is probably more than a coincidence. Hop plants are either male or female but only the female plants are cultivated because only they bear the distinctive cone-shaped green flowers that yield the elements that have proved so essential for brewing beer.

The active ingredients in hops are resins, oils and tannins. The first of these, the resins, are the ones that supply the bitterness. In fact there are two useful types of resin in the hop flower, humulones (alpha acids) and lupulones (beta acids). Of these, by far the most important are the humulones as they provide nearly all of the bittering power of the hops. This level of bitterness varies greatly from one variety of hop to another and is usually expressed as the percentage by weight of alpha acids in the hop cones. Thus a strongly bitter hop like Northern Brewer will be rated at between 7 and 10% (bitterness also varies from one crop to another) while a milder hop like Hallertauer Mittelfrüh will come in at 3–5%. The level of bitterness of a batch of hops will usually be printed on the container in which they are packaged. For commercial breweries that still use whole hop cones, the hops are usually packaged not according to the weight of the hops but according to the total alpha acids in the package, so the brewer knows exactly how much alpha acid he is putting into his batch of beer at any one time.

The following table lists some of the most widely used hops available today with their average AA ratings.

ALPHA-ACID RATINGS
European hop varieties

Aroma hops

Saaz	3
Tettnang	4
Spalt	4
Hallertauer Mittelfrüh	3.5
Styrian Golding	5
Perle	6.5
Kent Golding	5
Fuggles	4

Bittering hops

Northern Brewer	7.6
Nugget	9.6
Target	10
Brewer's Gold	6
Challenger	7

American hop varieties
Aroma hops
Goldings	5
Mt Hood	3.5
Willamette	5.5
Cascade	5.8

Bittering hops
Chinook	11.7
Galena	11.4
Nugget	11.7

Australasian hop varieties
Aroma hops
New Zealand Hallertauer	9

Bittering hops
Pride of Ringwood	9
Super Alpha	13.8
Sticklebract	14

Just how much in the way of Alpha Acid Units (AAU) the brewer puts into his beer depends on what kind of beer he is brewing. Generally speaking, the stronger a beer, the more bitterness it needs. Strong beers use more fermentable sugars and are therefore likely to be sweeter than lighter beers so they need that extra bitterness to balance them out. However, like all general rules, there are many exceptions to this one, and two beers of the same strength can have quite different levels of bitterness. German pilsener and Munich helles are both pale beers of around the average alcoholic strength of 5% alc/vol (4% alc/wt), yet the bitterness level of a pilsener can be as much as one-third higher than that of a helles because pilsener is traditionally a dry, hoppy style whereas helles, without being at all sweet, emphasises the smoothness of the malt flavours. In the same way, an English bitter, while often around the same strength and colour as a Scottish heavy, is likely to be considerably more bitter simply because the respective drinkers have come to expect it that way and their tastes have become accustomed to it. Belgian strong ales, which break most of the rules anyway, may rate at around 9% alc/vol (8% alc/wt) but seldom show any great bitterness.

In theory a brewer can choose to bitter his beer with a small quantity of high-alpha hops or a large quantity or low-alpha hops, but the equation is not as simple as it seems. As well as bitterness, hops, through their essential oils, also provide flavour and aroma; the catch is that the most bitter hops tend to provide the least pleasant or effective aroma. Thus the low-alpha varieties like Hallertauer, Saaz and others are often described as aroma hops whereas the high-alpha hops like Northern Brewer, Bullion and Australia's Pride of Ringwood are generally known as bittering hops. Add to this the fact that, in the first place, aroma hops are often more expensive than high-alpha varieties and, in the second, that the brewer has to use much more of them to get his target bitterness level, and the whole business becomes a complex exercise in balancing costs against benefits. The most common compromise struck by brewers of quality beer is to use bittering hops for bitterness and aroma hops for aroma.

This seems no more than common sense but it can be done only because of the way the different qualities are extracted from the hops. The alpha acids found in hops are not readily soluble at normal temperatures. They have first to be isomerised, that is, turned into soluble iso-alpha acids, and that starts to happen when the wort in which they are infusing is boiled. After about 45 minutes to an hour of boiling, most of the bitterness will have been extracted from them and they will have done their work. However, most of the other compounds that give hops their particular character are highly volatile and will not only dissolve very quickly into the boiling wort but will in fact be boiled off in the steam that rises from the kettle. So by boiling hops for an hour, which is fairly normal practice, you will get bitterness but little character out of them.

The solution is to boil the majority of hops for that hour but then add a smaller portion for only the last part of the boil. How long you put them in for will determine, to a certain extent, what characteristics you get from them. If you boil them for 15 minutes, you will extract a small amount of bitterness and save some of the hop flavour character. Shorter boiling times will give less and less bitterness and more and more of the volatile characteristics. To impart hop aroma to the beer, this final portion must be added as late as possible; some brewers add it just as the boil is being stopped, others run the hot wort on its way to the cooler through a container called a hop-back filled with fresh hops so the wort will pick up no more than an infusion of the most volatile hop oils. Finally, there is a technique called dry-hopping in which the aroma hops are never heated but are added to the fermenter, after the wort has been cooled and pitched with yeast, and left to steep for a week or more. This is a technique much used in Britain and the United States but forbidden to German brewers whose rules stipulate that the hops must be 'cooked' in the wort, if only for the shortest of periods.

Hops can be used in their more or less natural state, that is, in the form of loose cones, or they can be processed and used in more and more refined forms. The first processing step that can be taken by the hop grower or trader is to simply press the cones into large blocks. This does little to change their form or method of usage because they spring apart into separate cones again as soon as they touch liquid, but it makes them more compact for transportation. A development of that is the hop plug, a more compressed form of block usually formed into units of about 15 g ($\frac{1}{2}$ oz). At the time of writing, not many varieties are available in this form. The next stage is to crush them into a rough powder and press them into small pellets that look like green cat or poultry food. This greatly cuts down the size of the packaging and by reducing the surface area exposed to the air in storage may also help decrease the oxidisation of the resins and oils. Oxidisation is the main enemy of the brewer and hop dealer as it rapidly decreases the bittering power of the hops. Most of the important varieties are available in this form.

FIGURE 12.4
Hop cones
THE HOP ATLAS 1994,
JOH. BARTH & SOHN,
NUREMBERG

Increasing numbers of commercial brewers now use even more refined products such as hop extracts. These, as the name suggests, are liquid extracts containing the essential components of the hop which are leached out in a process using liquid carbon dioxide. The claim is that CO_2 does not react with any of the hop chemicals so their integrity is preserved. The advantage hop extracts have for a big brewer is that they are easier to store and handle, they can be added at a later stage in the brewing process, late in the boil, and they allow brewers to keep a tighter control over what is going into their beer. The disadvantages are, as with any form of reduction of an ingredient, that some characteristics are lost and that means the beer is likely to lose some character as well. However, there is no doubt that good beer can still be made with hop extracts, as the big Warsteiner brewery in Germany proves. Although its critics accuse its beer of blandness and lack of character, there is no suggestion that it is anything other than a well-made beer. It is also the single most successful beer in Germany, which is probably the most quality-conscious market in the world, so that must mean something.

Next come isomerised hop extracts. These are extracts in which the alpha acids are chemically isomerised, that is, turned into iso-alpha acids which will dissolve and impart bitterness into a cold wort. These offer the brewer the huge advantage that they do not have to be boiled in the wort and thus give even more control over levels of bitterness in the beer. A further refinement of these extracts are known as tetrahydro-iso alpha acids, hop extracts which have been chemically treated in such a way that they protect beer against spoilage caused by light rays, allowing brewers to bottle their beer in green or even clear bottles with less risk of damage. An added side benefit is that they aid head retention, which again looks good when the drinker is swigging straight from a clear bottle. Once again, in all this processing most of the individual hop character is lost but for mass-

FIGURE 12.6
Bottle of Warsteiner pilsener
WARSTEINER

market beers this is a price the brewers (and, it would appear, the public) are prepared to pay. And pay they do, for tetras are among the most expensive of all hop products.

Using hops in home brewing

While hop character and aroma in a beer are important in lifting the beer above the ordinary, they will be of little use unless the bitterness is at the right level in the first place to balance the malt and to fit in with the style you are brewing. Bitterness levels in beer are measured according to two almost identical scales, International Bitterness Units and European Brewing Convention. This book uses IBUs, as that is the traditional scale in use in the major home-brewing regions of North America, Britain and Australasia. IBUs can be measured if you have the right equipment but the technique is well beyond the capacity of the home brewer. However, the level of bitterness in a beer can be predicted from the quantity of hops going into the boil, their AAU level, the gravity of the wort and the length of the boil. The best way of doing this is to obtain a home-brewing recipe formulation program for your computer and let it calculate everything for you. Such programs are not particularly expensive, around US $100, and trial versions can be downloaded from the web site The Brewery. Also available on that site is a simple program just for calculating IBUs. It's called Tinibuw and it's free. Failing that, here is a very simplified and very approximate method of calculating the likely bitterness level of a beer in IBUs.

For 22.5 litres of a wort of 1.045 gravity, the formula is:

$$H = B \times 9.3/A$$
where
H = the required quantity of hops in grams
B = the required IBU level
A = the AAU rating of the hops.
This assumes a boil of at least 60 minutes.

So, if you have a wort of an original gravity of 1.045, your hops are rated at 10 AAU and you want a final bitterness level of 22 IBU, the calculation is:

$$22 \times 9.3/10 = 20.46 \text{ grams}$$

For a US 5-gallon wort of 1.045 gravity, the formula is:

$$H = B \times 8/A \times 28$$

These calculations will give you a rough idea of the bitterness levels you can expect from a given formulation. Higher-gravity worts will give less bitterness, lower gravities more bitterness, so bear that in mind when planning a recipe. Hop pellets are also a little more concentrated than loose cones so you should use about 10 per cent less of them. They also assume that the hops you are using are fresh and actually still able to yield the rate of AAUs stated on the package, a figure that refers to their AAU content at the time of packing.

Both cones and pellets have their strong supporters among home brewers. Certainly if you cannot find a supply of really fresh cones you would probably do better to look at pellets, for it seems to be generally accepted that they keep a little better—though, like most things to do with hops, this has proved difficult to prove. Whichever you do use, you should store them if possible in the freezer as low temperatures inhibit oxidisation. In fact, the question of whether you use cones or pellets is likely to be dictated more by the process you use when brewing, particularly how you separate the hops from the wort. In some methods the hop cones themselves act as a filter bed which traps the proteins, which are precipitated out into the wort during boiling and form a sludgy bed known as *trub* at the bottom of the kettle. In other methods the wort is drawn off from a tap or siphon well above the bottom of the kettle so the remains of the hop pellets, which also form a thick sludge, can be left behind in the boiler with the trub.

Just how bitter you make your beer depends on the style you are trying to brew but most styles have a fairly wide range of tolerances within which you can fit your own personal taste. The specifications in the individual recipes will give you the figures you need if you are a mash brewer; if you are brewing with extract kits you are largely at the mercy of the kit manufacturer although, with experience, you can make subsequent batches of the same brew a little more bitter by adding extra hops and boiling a little longer. It is, of course, impossible to remove bitterness from a can kit though you can make the final taste less perceptibly bitter by adding more malt extract and changing the balance of the finished beer. However, since can kits tend to be under-hopped if anything, this should hardly ever be necessary.

Storing hops

The biggest problem with keeping hops is that they tend to go stale if left exposed to the air as the alpha acids that are the important bittering agents oxidise. Oxidised alpha acids are far less effective at yielding bitterness so any calculations you make based on the bitterness figure when packed will be well astray. This means two things for the home brewer—don't buy too big a supply of hops at one time, and store what you have carefully. The lower the temperature the less the risk of oxidisation so keep them in the freezer at all times.

FIGURE 12.7
Filling old-style wooden kegs.
KÜPPERS BREWERY ARCHIVE, KÖLN

Yeast—the engine room of beer

Although beer has been brewed for possibly 10 000 years, it is only in the last 200 or so that we have really begun to understand just what it is that turns a sweet liquid into the fermented drink we know as beer. The answer, of course, is yeast.

Yeast is a living creature, a unicellular organism and a member of the fungus family. There are hundreds of different yeasts in nature and they can be found virtually everywhere there is life. From a brewer's point of view, however, most of them are at best useless and at worst disastrous. With a few notable exceptions, all they will do to a brew is turn it into vinegar or worse.

Fortunately, over the centuries in which men and women have been brewing, they have isolated and identified a small number of yeasts whose behaviour can be predicted fairly accurately and have learned how best to use them. Each of these types has a number of different strains so the variety of yeasts available to the brewer is in practice quite large.

Essentially, yeast works by eating sugar and producing alcohol and carbon dioxide. When a yeast colony comes into contact with a solution of fermentable sugars, it immediately begins to consume the oxygen in the wort to provide itself with energy for the job that lies ahead. At the same time it starts multiplying rapidly. This stage is known as the aerobic or lag phase of fermentation.

Once up to optimum numbers, the yeast starts feeding on the sugars in the solution and in fact it will continue to feed on the sugars until it dies, either because it runs out of food or it has poisoned itself with its own waste product, alcohol. Sound familiar?

The basic cycle is as simple as that, yet the exact way it proceeds is slightly different for each variety of yeast, which is why different yeasts brew such widely different beers and why brewers, having found a yeast which works well for them, will guard it almost with their lives.

There are two basic types of brewers' yeasts and it is their basic differences that determine and delineate the two great families of beer styles—ales and lagers. Ale yeasts are often referred to as top-fermenting yeasts, not because they only work at the top of the brew but because traditionally they used to float to the top after they had done their work. Brewers would then skim them off the top of the wort and re-use them in the next brew. Lager yeasts are called bottom-fermenters because they have always sunk to the bottom of the brew after doing their work.

However, the situation is a little confused by the fact that there are now many top-fermenting yeasts which, after flocculating (forming into clumps) and rising, eventually drop through the brew and end up on the bottom in the same way as a bottom-fermenter. Most commercial top-fermenters in fact behave in this fashion; they have replaced the older classic styles for two reasons—it is easier to collect them off the bottom of the brew after it has been drained from the fermenter rather than go through the business of continually skimming them off the top; and, because they drop out more quickly and thoroughly, they also tend to make for a clearer beer, which saves time and money on filtration.

However, there is another vitally important, in fact crucial, difference between the two types of yeast. Top-fermenters work best at temperatures between 15 and 22°C (60–72°F); bottom-fermenters operate most effectively between 8 and 14°C (46–57°F).

These different fermentation temperatures, added to slight differences in the types of sugars they will and will not ferment, result in big differences in the kind of beer that is produced. Warm fermentation brings out esters that give the resulting beers a slightly acid fruitiness; cold fermentation emphasises the mildly sulphury flavours which, in very low concentrations, give a clean crispness to the finished product and that classic European flavour. It's a difference which is easy to prove to yourself by tasting first a German or Czech lager, then trying a British bitter.

FIGURE 12.8
Modern fermentation equipment and techniques
FULLER SMITH & TURNER PLC

FIGURE 12.9
Reinhardt Krätsch at his traditional Sünner Kölsch brewery in Köln
LAURIE STRACHAN

This temperature difference is carried over to the way the beer is served. British warm-fermented ales have to be served at a temperature high enough for the gentle esters to be appreciated. Chill them too much and these subtleties will disappear. So British beer is ideally served at around 10°C (50°F). European beers should be served somewhat cooler, but not too cold, for they too have subtleties that will be killed by over-chilling. A serving temperature of around 6–7°C (43–45°F) is about right for them.

In other parts of the world, beer is served a good deal colder. Probably the extreme is found in Australia where the beer often comes out of the taps at what would be near freezing point if it weren't for the fact that alcohol has a lower freezing point than water. It's hard to say which came first, but it could explain why Australian beer is not noted for its subtlety.

All brewing used to be done using top-fermenting yeasts; nowadays the situation is reversed and at least 90 per cent of brewing across the world is done with lager yeasts. The change came about in the middle of the nineteenth century when Bavarian brewers discovered that, when they stored their beer in Alpine caves to mature, it stabilised and the yeast dropped out to the bottom of the storage vessels. According to legend, a Bavarian monk took this new, mutated yeast to Pilsen in Bohemia, founding the great tradition of pilsener beer. More factually, a Danish brewer called Jacobsen carried some of the yeast across Europe to Denmark, where it was set to work in the great Carlsberg brewery in Copenhagen.

Studies were made of this yeast and it was isolated to a pure culture, appropriately known as *Saccharomyces carlsbergensis*, although nowadays it is more commonly known as *Saccharomyces uvarum*. Top-fermenting yeasts, which are still being used extensively in Britain and Belgium and

FIGURE 12.10

Modern yeasts can recapture the authentic German flavours produced by traditional breweries such as the historic Warsteiner brewery

WARSTEINER

parts of Germany where alt (old) beer is brewed, go under the biological name of *Saccharomyces cerevisiae*, from the Latin *cerevisia* ('beer'), which is itself derived from the name of the goddess of grain, Ceres.

It is this divide between warm and cold fermentations by which we categorise the world of beer. Beers made by warm top-fermentation go under the heading of ales; those made by cold fermentation are usually referred to as lagers. Within those categories, there are many further divisions and some downright oddities that go to make up the huge variety of styles that make up the world of beer.

13 Methods

Brewing a full-mash beer

The way brewers make beer has changed only in detail over the past few hundred years—because it is the only way to make beer. It consists of five steps: mashing, sparging, boiling, cooling and fermenting. Commercial brewers and some home brewers carry out the entire process, but most home brewers leave the first two or three steps to be done commercially then take over from there.

In order to make beer, our aim is to convert the starches in malted grain into soluble sugars and dissolve them out into the wort. We do this by steeping the malt, and any adjuncts we may be using, in hot water and leaving it for between 30 minutes and two hours while enzymes in the malted grains go to work changing the starches to sugars.

FIGURE 13.1
Equipment changes, but the principles of beer-making remain the same; a scene from a German brewery in 1903
BEHRINGER, *LÖWENBRÄU*, MUNICH 1991, P. 164

(Adjuncts are the unmalted ingredients that brewers sometimes use to lighten or thicken the flavour and body of their beer, to reduce the chances of chill haze or simply because they happen to be cheap in that particular geographical area. They include such things as unmalted barley, rice, wheat and maize.)

When we mix malted grains with water at the right temperature, between 63 and 70°C (145–160°F), we activate enzymes in the malt which convert the starches in the malt to soluble sugars. There are two enzymes involved, alpha and beta amylase—but, as they work so closely together, they are often known collectively as 'diastase'. Alpha amylase breaks up long strings of starch molecules into shorter chunks of unfermentable sugars called dextrins; beta amylase then further breaks up most of these chunks, turning them into a fermentable sugar called maltose. A proportion of dextrins remains unconverted to maltose and, because they cannot be fermented by most brewing yeasts, they remain in the beer and give it its body and mouthfeel.

For a good beer of average body, the proportion of these sugars in the wort should be roughly 25 per cent dextrins and 75 per cent maltose. For a thicker, heavier body we need more dextrins, for a lighter beer, more maltose.

Beta amylase works best at a temperature of around 55°C (131°F) while alpha operates best at 66°C (150°F). In practice, if we hold the mash at a steady temperature of around 65°C (150°F), they will work together and produce an average 25/75 wort.

Because the two enzymes do their best work at differing temperatures, it follows that we can alter the kind of wort they produce by changing the temperature of the mash. If we want a wort with a higher proportion of dextrins in it—which, in turn, will give us a beer with more body for a given alcoholic strength—we need to run the mash at a slightly higher temperature, say 66–68°C (150–154°F). Because the beta amylase does not work so well at these higher temperatures it will not break down so much of the wort into maltose, leaving more dextrins in it. As the dextrins are not fermentable by beer yeasts, they will still be left in the beer after fermentation and the result will be a beer with a heavier body. On the other hand, if we are looking for a lighter-bodied, easy-drinking beer, then we can mash at a lower temperature, say 63–64°C (145–147°F), and produce a wort with fewer dextrins and more maltose.

Bear in mind that a beer with a higher proportion of dextrins will not ferment out as far as a lighter-bodied beer and so will in fact produce less alcohol for a given amount of fermentables. So, if we want a strong, full-bodied beer we must use a good deal more malt.

If we are using grain adjuncts we must also consider that they usually contain few or no conversion enzymes. That simply means they must be mashed together with enough malt for the enzymes in the malt to do the work. Malt varies in its enzymatic content depending on grain variety and how it has been malted. If you are in doubt about what proportion of adjuncts your malt will be able to mash, consult your supplier; otherwise keep the proportion of adjuncts in the mash below 10 per cent.

Preparing the grains

Before you mash the grains, they must first be ground, or cracked. The objective is not to grind them to a flour—that would result in all sorts of technical problems later in the process when you come to straining the liquid off the grains—but just to crack the shells and break up the kernels enough to let the hot water into them where it can activate the enzymes.

Most home brew stores sell grain in ready-cracked form so you just have to add it straight to the hot water. However, if you find you are doing lots of mashing, you might think of buying whole malt in bulk and grinding it yourself with one of the many home-brewing grain mills now on the market. Bulk malt can often be bought for around a third of the price of pre-cracked packaged malt and the long-term saving can be considerable.

Any adjuncts or specialty malts you intend to use should be cracked where necessary then added to the mash with the rest of the grains.

Methods of mashing

Commercial brewers use three different techniques of mashing—the infusion mash, the step mash, or upward infusion, and the decoction mash. Of these, the infusion mash is the most suitable method for home brewers because it is the simplest—but we will look at the others because some brewers consider there are compelling reasons for using them.

THE INFUSION MASH For this method of mashing we simply mix a measured amount of grain with a measured amount of water heated to a predetermined temperature and leave the resulting porridge alone while the enzymes go to work.

The table opposite gives some approximate quantities to use in order to ensure that the mash settles out at around 67–68°C (153–154°F). It's probably better to aim for a starting temperature higher than 65°C (150°F) simply because the mash will lose some heat as it sits.

Columns 1 and 2 are the amount of grain you will be mashing; columns 3 and 4 the amount of water you will need in the mash tun. In practice it is handy to have a kettle of boiling water handy to add to the mash in case you have to adjust the temperature upwards. To adjust it downwards, just add cold water.

Conversion should take place within an hour but some brewers prefer to allow it to go on longer in the belief that they will get a higher yield of sugars from the grain or that the finished beer will have fewer problems with hazes. I mash for two hours because experience has told me that the whole thing seems to work better that way.

Grain		Mash water at 77°C (170°F)	
kg	lbs	Litres	US gal
3.0	5.5	7.0	1.3
3.5	6.4	8.5	1.6
4.0	7.3	10.0	1.9
4.5	8.3	11.5	2.1
5.0	9.2	13.0	2.4
5.5	10.1	14.5	2.7

The ideal vessel in which to do an infusion mash is the everyday picnic cooler, known in Australia as an Esky. Like the insulated mash tuns of commercial British brewers, it will keep the mash at a reasonably stable temperature for the one or two hours necessary. Failing this, some brewers use a large cooking pot in which they heat the mash on the stove and then, when it is at the desired temperature, wrap it in something like a blanket or quilt to help it retain heat. The advantage of this is that they can give the mash a heat boost halfway through to bring it back up to the required temperature. The third alternative is the Bruheat-style boiler, which is simply a strong food-grade polythene bin of 25 litres (7 gallons) or so to which has been fitted an immersion heating element. This can be set by thermostat to hold the correct temperature but has to be watched to make sure it doesn't overheat.

THE STEP MASH The simple infusion mash works well with most of the standard malts a home brewer will encounter. However, some brewers prefer to do a mash that involves starting at a lower temperature then raising the mash to the conversion or saccharification temperature. There are two main reasons for this.

The first is that barley is not malted in the same way everywhere, nor are all barleys the same. Most of the malts encountered by home brewers are what we call highly modified and can be mashed by the simple, one-temperature infusion mash. However some malts, particularly European malts, are less modified.

With under-modified malts, the mash has to be put through a preliminary stage or stages (known as rests) before it goes into the saccharification stage.

In the simplest form of step mash, the grains are first mashed in at a relatively low temperature, usually around 55°C (131°F), then left for a rest of 20 minutes. This is known as the protein rest as it breaks down proteins in the malt and makes them more suitable for saccharification. The mash temperature is then raised to around 65°C (150°F) and the mash is left for 30 minutes to an hour for conversion to sugars.

A second reason for doing a step mash, even with well-modified malts, is that it slightly increases the yield of sugars from the grain, although the increase is probably no more than about 1 or 2 per cent. In a giant brewing

Grain		Mash water at 70°C (158°F)		Added boiling water	
kg	lbs	litres	US gal	litres	US gal
3	5.5	6.5	1.2	3.2	0.6
3.5	6.4	7.5	1.4	3.7	0.7
4	7.3	8.5	1.6	4.2	0.8
4.5	8.3	9.5	1.8	4.7	0.9
5	9.2	10.5	1.9	5.2	1.0

system, this adds up to a considerable cost saving over the year; in a home-brewing situation, it hardly seems worth the trouble.

A further step is often taken, raising the mash temperature to 77°C (170°F), mainly to make the mash less viscous and more free-running, and therefore maximise the yield of sugars. This step must be done by applying heat directly to the mash and so cannot be done if you are using a mash tun without any means of applying heat.

Once again though, there is little evidence that this is worth the trouble in home-brewing situations.

The mash temperature can be raised either by applying heat to the mash or by adding boiling water. The advantage of the addition method is that you can use the same kind of picnic cooler used for the simple infusion mash, and there is no risk of scorching the wort. The problem is that the mash becomes very liquid unless you start with a thicker mash in the first place. So, for this kind of mash either the Bruheat or cooking-pot systems have definite advantages.

For those who wish to try it, here are some quantities for a simple, two-step mash using the addition method of raising the temperature.

It is always safer to underestimate the amount of boiling water you add to the mash to raise its temperature. You can always add more if the settling temperature is not high enough.

THE DECOCTION MASH The decoction mash has been traditionally used by European brewers as a means of taking the mash up two or three temperature steps; some brewers believe it helps give lagers more of a European-style flavour profile and draws a richer malt flavour from the grains.

It involves mashing-in at low temperature then draining off measured portions of the mash, boiling them and adding them back into the mash to raise the temperature. The temperature steps can be the same as in the step mash, but the most complicated method, the triple decoction, involves mashing-in at room temperature and raising the temperature in steps from there. The main drawbacks of this method are that it takes a lot of extra work and time and that it is easy to scorch the portions of the mash as you boil them.

Again, the advantages of this method for home brewers are marginal, but here are some quantities for a simple single decoction. The grain should be mashed in at 55°C (131°F) and the mash left to rest for at least 20 minutes. Next remove about a third of the total mash and boil it for about 15 minutes, stirring constantly to prevent burning. Return it to the main mash, check that the temperature is within the saccharification range you are aiming for, then leave the mash to sit for a further 20 minutes. If you wish to mash out at 77°C (170°F), carry out

Grain		Mash water at 67°C (153°F)	
kg	lbs	litres	US gal
3	5.5	7	1.3
3.5	6.4	8.5	1.6
4	7.3	10	1.9
4.5	8.3	11.5	2.1
5	9.2	13	2.4

the same process, removing and boiling a third of the mash then returning it to the tun.

As the main mash itself is not heated, any of the mash tun systems described above can be used for a decoction mash.

SPARGING

After you have completed your mash program, the next stage in brewing is to drain the hot, sweet wort off the grains and rinse the grist out with further hot water to collect as much of the fermentable material as is reasonably possible. This is known as sparging. For this you need either to have a mash tun fitted with some means of straining off the liquid or a separate sparging vessel. British practice is to use a mash tun with a false bottom riddled with small holes and fitted with a tap. When the mash is finished, the liquid is drained off through the tap and the grains are left behind on the false bottom.

On the other hand, in Europe, where it is the custom to use the mash tun also as the boiler or kettle, the entire mash once completed is transferred to a separate sparging vessel known as a lauter tun. The grains are transferred to this tun which has a false bottom and drain tap and the liquid is drawn off. In both methods the next step is the same, further hot water being sprayed on top of the grains to wash the remaining sugars through.

Home brewers can use either method. It is possible to buy insulated mash tuns—cylindrical picnic coolers fitted with a false bottom and tap—but cheaper to pick up a 20-litre polythene bucket of the type used extensively in the food industry, and fit that with the false bottom and tap, making it an effective lauter tun. You must then work out some way of steadily spraying around 18 litres (4 gallons) of hot water on top of your grains—but again, help is at hand. A company, Listerman Mfg, produces a range of inexpensive accessories for mashing, including a very neat false bottom that fits into various sizes of polythene bucket or cylindrical cooler, and a sparging set-up that sprays the sparge water in a controllable flow onto the grains.

The amount of sparge water used is not critical. Around 20 litres (3.7 US gallons) should be sufficient for up to 5 kg (9.2 lbs) of grain (see Preface). Theoretically you should use more sparge water as the amount of grain increases, but in practice this will produce too much collected wort and is difficult to work with unless you have a very large boiler in which the wort can be boiled down to the batch size, as is done in commercial breweries. Bear in mind that most of the sugars are drained out early in the sparge, and towards the end the amount of fermentables being extracted is getting smaller and smaller, so cutting the mash short will not lose you too much and will save time and effort.

THE BOIL

Next the wort has to be collected and boiled. Usually the wort is drained off from the mash or lauter tun straight into the boiler. A boiler is any vessel in which all the wort, all 22.5 litres (5 US gallons), can be heated to boiling point and kept there for at least an hour. Many home brewers use large cooking pots and heat them directly on the stove; some use old brewery kegs that have been cut open at the top and heat them on special high-power gas burners. Yet others use the Bruheat-style immersion heater; it is big enough to hold the entire wort and it will stand up to boiling for hours. It usually has the added advantage of having a tap fitted to it that makes it easier to transfer the cooled wort to the fermenter.

The purposes of boiling are first to sterilise the wort, killing off any bacteria or wild yeasts that may have been in the grains in the first place, secondly to infuse it with hop bitterness and flavour, and thirdly to precipitate out haze-causing proteins.

At the start of the boil it is time to add the bittering hops, and here again there are different ways to approach this step. It must be borne in mind that the hops have to be removed from the wort at the end of the boil before transferring the wort to the fermenter. So before you start you must have some way worked out of removing them. The simplest way is to place the hops in a loose-weave bag known, not surprisingly, as a hop bag, and boil them in the wort in the bag, rather like using a big tea bag which can be lifted out at the end of the boil. The only problem with this method is that it makes late hop additions a little more difficult as you have to have a separate bag for each one.

To remove the hops, professionals use a hop-back, a special filtering device through which the wort is passed before it is cooled; a simple strainer can also be used. However, this step must be done before the wort is cooled otherwise there is a risk of the wort picking up contamination from the equipment, and thus this method will only work if you have an external wort cooler, of which more in a moment.

My method is to use a Bruheat-style boiler with a simple trick that mimics the function of a hop-back but removes the risk of infection. Before I start filling the boiler, I take a small, stainless-steel pot-scourer and jam it into the tap-housing on the inside of the boiler bucket, making sure that it is firmly lodged. As it is immersed in the boiling liquid, the steel-wool mesh will be completely sterilised; then when running the wort out of the boiler into the fermenter, it will act as a strainer, preventing the hops from blocking up the tap. The spent hops will pile up around this improvised strainer and, as the wort passes through them, the bed of hops will, in turn, filter out the protein residues or 'trub', which will by then have been precipitated out into the wort by the boiling then cooling, leaving the beer potentially cleaner and purer. The great advantages of this system are that several doses of hops can be added at various times in order to get the desired characteristics of the style I am brewing—and the hops are boiled loose in the boiler liquid, enabling potentially better extraction of their bitterness. It is believed by many brewers that a third possible benefit of boiling hops loose is that the action of their movement through the wort helps precipitate out the trub.

In commercial breweries the wort is usually boiled for somewhere between one and two hours, during which time the liquid is kept at a strong, rolling boil. I boil for around 70 minutes and this seems to be sufficient time for the proteins to come out of solution and form small, whitish flakes in the wort. This is usually known as the 'hot break', and it is a very important consideration when working out how long you should boil. While virtually all the hop bitterness will be extracted in around 45 minutes, you can add your bittering hops at the very start of the boil for the sake of convenience as a little extra boiling is unlikely to do them or the beer any harm.

Flavour and aroma hops are added at the times specified in the recipes, calculating back from the finishing time. Once the aroma hops have been added, the boiler, or whatever heat source is being used to boil it, must be switched off and cooling should begin as soon as possible.

To aid in precipitating out the trub it helps to add a teaspoonful of Irish moss, a preparation of dried seaweed whose gelatinous properties help the flakes of trub to flocculate together and therefore clear more quickly. The Irish moss should be added around 30 minutes before the end of the boil.

COOLING

The next step after boiling is to cool the wort down to a temperature low enough to pitch the yeast. This should be done as quickly as possible for two reasons. In the first place, if the wort is cooled slowly there will be a long period during which it is a little too hot to pitch a yeast, yet cool enough for some bacteria to get into it and start to multiply. In the second, the faster the wort is cooled the more proteins are precipitated out in a second reaction called the 'cold break', which sees the small flakes of the hot break flocculate or clump together into larger particles which sink more readily to the bottom of the wort.

Most modern commercial breweries cool the wort by passing it through a plate heat-exchanger, though some still use the older style of counter-flow chiller. This is, in effect, a long, narrow, coiled pipe that is surrounded by another, wider pipe in which cold water is flowing. The water flows in the opposite direction to the wort hence the description 'counter-flow'. Home brewers can use this technique too and a number of models of small counter-flow chiller are available, mainly from the United States. The disadvantage of this approach is the need to have the chiller completely sanitised before the wort is passed through it, which can be difficult.

For most home brewers it is probably more convenient to use an immersion chiller. This is no more than a length of copper tubing bent into a coil narrow enough to fit into the boiler. At each end is attached a length of ordinary garden hose. The coil is first cleaned on the outside with hot water to remove any loose dirt, then it is immersed in the boiler, from five to ten minutes before the end of the boil, to sterilise it. The hose at one end is attached to the cold tap, the other end sits in the sink. As soon as the boiler's heating element has been switched off, cold water from the tap is run through the coil as it sits in the boiler. In this way the coil acts as a heat exchanger. The cold water running through it picks up the heat of the wort and takes it with it down the sink. It takes no more than 30 minutes, even in an Australian heatwave, to get the wort down to a temperature of around 21°C (70°F), which is cool enough to pitch even a lager yeast.

If you are unwilling to invest in some sort of cooler until you are quite sure you will be using it enough to justify the cost, the next best solution is to immerse the entire boiler in a bath of cold, preferably running, water and wait until it cools. This may take several hours, however—and it can't be done if you are using a plastic bucket with an immersion heater, as the water will get into the electrical connections and ruin them.

Whatever method you use to cool your wort, you should aim to get it down at least to 25°C (75°F) for an ale, or perhaps 21°C (70°F) for a lager, before you think of starting the next stage, fermentation.

Brewing with a can kit

As we have seen, the brewing process is simple enough. Malted barley is steeped in hot water until the starches in it turn to sugars and are leached out. That's called 'mashing', and the resultant liquid is called the 'sweet wort'. This wort is then boiled with the flowers of hop plants until it is infused with bitterness and hop flavour. It is then 'bitter wort'. The bitter wort is cooled and yeast is added. Over the next few days, the yeast converts most of the sugars in the wort to alcohol and carbon dioxide. Effectively, you then have beer, though there are further processes of clarification, and sometimes secondary fermentation, before the beer is packaged and consumed.

It's quite possible to do all of those steps in a home situation, and some of us do. However, the great majority of home brewers don't go to all this trouble. Most of them buy made-up kits and start from there. A kit usually consists of a can of malt extract syrup plus a package of dried yeast. The syrup is in effect a condensed bitter wort. The manufacturer has taken the steps of mashing, boiling and concentrating the wort, leaving you merely to add water and plain white sugar, pitch your packet of yeast and wait for it to go to work.

It's simple, and it can be done in about 20 minutes, but there's a catch. In the first place, the business of concentrating the wort, no matter how carefully it is done, always has the effect of removing some of its original properties. So the resulting beer doesn't quite taste the same as the real thing. It's rather like the difference between freshly ground coffee and instant.

Secondly, adding a kilogram (2.2 lbs) of white sugar, as most can kits recommend, will raise the alcohol level of the beer but won't do much for the flavour. Most straightforward can-kit beers have a sourish, almost cidery flavour, little hop character and a thin body. Notwithstanding this, there are an awful lot of people who like their beer that way, as witness the number of cans that move off the shelves of home brew shops and supermarkets every day.

However, there is a method of brewing that retains the simplicity of the can kit but produces a much better end product. It simply involves substituting other ingredients in place of some or all of the sugar and, if you want to take it a little further, using a better yeast that the dried variety that comes with the can. That's the approach that is favoured in the recipes you will find later in this book.

You can buy can kits from a supermarket but you'll get a much bigger selection from your local home-brew shop. You'll need to go there anyway to buy some of the basic equipment needed for the job, and for the extra ingredients. However, most of what you need will already be there in your kitchen—things like pots or kettles to heat the water, wooden spoons to stir and, of course, a can opener.

There are possibly thousands of different can kits on the market and they cover virtually every known style. Exactly which kit you buy will depend on the style you are brewing and what your supplier carries. It is not within the scope of this, or any, book to review every can kit on the market; there are too many of them and they change quite regularly. Bear in mind that the most expensive are not necessarily the best and the cheapest not necessarily the worst. Try to find other home brewers whose beer you have tasted and liked, and ask them what they recommend. A reliable home-brew supplier should also be able to steer you in the right direction.

You will need something in which to ferment your beer. In theory, this can be any sort of large container, like a garbage bin, that's big enough to hold the 22 litres (US 5 gallons) of malt extract and water that you will be using; however, I would strongly recommend that you buy a container made or properly adapted for the purpose. Home-brew shops sell food-grade plastic buckets fitted with a lid, a tap and an airlock ready for you to start brewing. In the United States many brewers use the 5-gallon glass carboys which are readily available there. They have the advantage of being easier to keep really clean than plastic but the disadvantage of not having taps fitted. This simply means you will have to siphon liquids out with a suitable length of plastic hose. Fittings to make siphoning easier are also available at home-brew stores.

The can kit will come with a set of instructions, either on the can itself or in a leaflet tucked under a tightly fitting lid. The method varies little from can to can. Stand the can in a pot of very hot water for about 10 to 20 minutes to soften the contents and ensure that it all pours out easily. While you are waiting, fill the fermenter with cold tap water to which you have added two teaspoons of ordinary household bleach. This should kill off most of the bugs which might be clinging unseen to the plastic and which could turn your beer to vinegar.

When the can is ready to go, drain the liquid from the fermenter and rinse it with cold water. Open the can and pour the contents into the fermenter. Add the extra ingredients and 2 litres (US 1 quart) of boiling water. Mix well until it has all dissolved into a thick syrup then add 20 litres of cold water. Add the yeast that comes with the can, put the lid on the fermenter and fit the airlock.

Most home-brew shops these days sell 'improver' kits designed precisely for the purpose of improving the flavour of the cans. They come under different names and your best bet is to ask the shopkeeper what exactly is in them.

Most of the can-kit recipes in this book specify exactly what extra ingredients should go into the brew in order to approximate the style you are trying to brew. Let's use as an example the recipe for brown ale on pages 124–5. This is based on a brown ale can kit with the 1 kilogram (2.2 lbs) of sugar called for in the instructions replaced by a mixture of 500 g (1.1 lbs) powdered malt extract and 500 g (1.1 lbs) malto-dextrin.

Powdered malt extract is made from a sweet (unhopped) wort that is condensed even further down than the syrup until it turns into fine crystals. Malto-dextrin is a mix of dextrose (glucose) with around 20 per cent of unfermentable dextrins; since these dextrins do not ferment right out, they replace some of the body that has been lost to the beer in the process of condensing the malt extract.

The other important source of character in beer is the hops. It is the balance between hop and malt flavours that makes for a good beer. Again, the manufacturer of the kit will have aimed for a hop–malt balance that will be right if the kit is made up using 1 kilogram (2.2 lbs) of sugar. When we add extra malt, we throw that balance out so we then have to correct it by adding more hops.

The easiest way to get the extra hop flavour into your brew is to add about 10 g (1/3 oz) of hop pellets (these are simply hop flowers ground up and compacted) after you add the boiling water. You won't get much bitterness out of them—that takes a long boil—but you should get some flavour and aroma. As for the pellets, they will disintegrate in the liquid and eventually sink to the bottom of the fermenter below the level of the tap, so you leave them behind when you bottle.

All this can be done in the fermenter itself but there is a better, though slightly longer, way. In order to give the kind of scope for variation that we need when attempting to brew specific styles, we need to add one step to the brewing of the can kit. For this we need a saucepan of at least 5 litres (US 4 quarts). Half fill the saucepan with hot tap water then add the powdered ingredients, whisking and stirring to mix them in and dissolve them. Next add the contents of the can and bring the whole thing to the boil. Add the flavouring hops and simmer for 10 to 15 minutes. Turn off the heat, add the aroma hops and stir once or twice. Now pour the contents of the saucepan into the fermenter.

It helps if you pour it through some sort of large strainer to remove the hop debris. If you don't have a big enough strainer and you are fermenting in a plastic bucket, you can make one from a pair of women's pantyhose. Tie off the legs as high as possible and cut them off below the ties. Boil the pantyhose for about 10 minutes to remove any dyes and they are ready to be used. The elastic waist of the pantyhose will fit neatly around the rim of the bucket and the fine mesh will filter out even the finest hop debris.

If you are adding only aroma hop pellets at the very end there will be no need to strain the wort as the small amount of hops involved will break down to a fine sludge and fall to the bottom of the fermenter, leaving the relatively clear beer to be poured off it when fermentation is over.

Another useful tip when brewing in this way is to have ready a block of ice to help cool the wort down to fermentation temperature. You can prepare this the day before by filling a sanitised plastic ice-cream container (or something similar) of around 2 litres (1 quart) with cold water and putting it in the freezer overnight. Unmould this large iceblock into the bottom of the fermenter before you pour in the hot wort.

Now fill the fermenter up to the required mark (22.5 litres or US 5 gallons) with cold tap water. Check that the temperature is below 25°C (77°F) before pitching your yeast. This whole process shouldn't take longer than around 30 to 40 minutes and it has two distinct advantages over the simpler method—first, you are boiling all the ingredients and so are less likely to pick up infections and off-flavours; secondly, you have more flexibility in adding extra hops.

This method of brewing will still not give you a close replica of one of the great beer styles but you will be surprised how good it can be given the right yeast and a good can kit.

Fermentation

The process of fermentation is the point at which the wort starts to turn into beer, which makes it perhaps the single most important and critical part of the whole brewing operation. Up to this point, it has been important only to be reasonably clean in everything you do; as soon as the wort has been cooled down to fermentation temperature *cleanliness becomes all-important*. A cooled wort is a highly desirable feast for bacteria and wild yeasts—and they lurk everywhere. In theory, everything that touches the beer should from this point on be sterile, but that is obviously quite impossible in a home or even in a big brewery situation.

The actual process of fermentation and the behaviour of yeasts were covered in the previous chapter; here we are concerned with the how rather than the why. The first thing we need is a container in which to ferment the beer. The choice of fermenter is not critical, as long as it is clean and easy to use. In most countries other than the United States, home brewers use food-grade plastic buckets with a capacity of around 26 litres (US 7 gallons). These can easily be fitted with an airtight lid and an airlock, and in fact can be bought already set up in this way from most home-brew shops. In the United States there is a ready supply of glass carboys with a capacity of US 5 gallons, from the days when water-coolers used glass bottles rather than plastic, and because glass is easier to get really clean than plastic it makes sense to use them for home brewing. As mentioned previously, the disadvantage of carboys is that they do not have taps, so liquids have to be transferred out of them by siphoning. That has not stopped US home brewers from becoming the most advanced of their kind in the world, however—and whole treatises on the art of siphoning have been published in US magazines and books. The carboy can be closed with a rubber stopper drilled with a hole in which an airlock can be fitted.

The first step towards fermentation is to transfer the cooled wort into the fermenter. It's a good idea to splash the liquid into the bottom of the fermenter as this aerates the wort, providing oxygen for the first, aerobic phase of yeast activity. If you can pitch your yeast at the same time as you are filling the fermenter, you will ensure that the yeast is well spread throughout the wort and in a good position to go to work. It is also important to pitch enough yeast into the wort to make sure it will get through its early, multiplying, lag phase as quickly as possible and start consuming the fermentable sugars. A quick, strong fermentation is one of the most important ways to keep a beer from developing infections and off-flavours, simply because an active, healthy, hungry yeast will out-consume any competitors, which will die of starvation before they can get a hold and start affecting the beer.

Just how much yeast you will need is hard to say because yeast comes in so many different forms. If you are using a dried yeast in the familiar 5 or 7 g packets, it is better to pitch two packets as more yeast means a quicker start to fermentation. The new dried yeasts like Safale and Saflager come in 11.5 g sachets, which are enough in themselves to ensure a vigorous start. Liquid yeasts will have to be cultured up according to the directions on the pack.

The easiest way to monitor the progress of fermentation is to check on the level of water in the airlock. As soon as the pressure from inside the fermenter starts to move the liquid down and round the bottom bend in the tube, you can be sure fermentation is under way. This can take up to 12 hours but six hours is a much better performance, and a yeast like Saflager will give you that easily.

Once started, the yeast will continue to indicate it is working by forcing gas (carbon dioxide) through the airlock until it has consumed all available fermentables, whereupon it will start to autolyse, or eat itself, until it dies out completely. However, we don't want it to go that far, because autolysed yeast can give a beer unpleasant flavours and also because we want it to keep working.

Fermentations are effectively divided into two phases, primary and secondary. The primary phase is considered to go on until between two-thirds and three-quarters of the fermentables have been consumed. At this point the action of the yeast begins to slow and it goes into the secondary phase. Brewers use these two phases carefully to get the best results from their beer.

After the primary fermentation is over, and that can take anything from three to seven days, the beer should be racked off the bulk of the yeast, which will have dropped to the bottom of the fermenter, and transferred to another vessel. However, timing is not critical and you can leave a beer on the yeast for an extra week if you wish or if you just don't have time to do the transfer.

At this point you have to decide whether you are going to lager the beer, or bottle or keg it straight away. If you decide to lager it, you should transfer it to another vessel and store it for two to four weeks at as close to 0°C (32°F) as you can manage. It's also preferable to use some kind of sealed pressure container so that, as the yeast continues its slow secondary fermentation, the CO_2 given off will be held within the container and will dissolve into the beer, giving it a light carbonation. This is the classic method of brewing lagers, still practised by some brewers in Germany and other parts of the world. You can then bottle the beer from the secondary vessel. This way you will get the least amount of yeast in each bottle, and a beer that is easier to keep clear.

On the other hand you can simply bottle or keg the beer after its primary fermentation. Each bottle then becomes a kind of miniature lagering tank. Store the bottles at close to 0°C (32°F) for at least two weeks, and preferably longer, before drinking. Much the same goes for kegs. They too should be stored at low temperature for as long as reasonably possible before the beer is served. Obviously the longer you leave the beer in lager, the clearer it is likely to be, but anything from four weeks onwards should be more than adequate.

Recipes for brewing the great beers

The recipes that follow are intended to make it possible for the home brewer to brew beer in some of the world's great styles. They represent, however, only one way of going about that and can be varied according to the individual's level of skill and knowledge—and the ingredients and processes readily available. The figures are given in metric for a 22.5-litre batch (the equivalent of the old 5 Imperial gallons), and for a US 5-gallon batch, so no further conversion is required.

14 How to use the recipes

Clearly the only way to really approximate a distinct style of beer is to brew it more or less the way the original brewers do or did—and that is by a full mash. However, there are millions of home brewers all over the world who have neither the desire nor the time to attempt this style of brewing. For them I have given a simplified form of recipe involving the use of a pre-prepared can kit with one or two suitable enhancements. I do not pretend this will give a particularly close approximation to the style being brewed but, given the right can kit, it will produce a drinkable beer of the general type we are aiming at.

When attempting to brew a beer to a particular style, it is important to know what you are aiming for. The first section of each recipe outlines this aim and goes into the different ways in which it can be achieved. The parameters that define a style are largely to do with alcoholic strength, colour and bitterness, and the range within which a beer should fall if it is to be considered as fitting into that style have been fairly drawn. Other characteristics, such as aroma and flavour, can be appreciated but not necessarily measured accurately, and certainly not without the kind of sophisticated equipment that is well beyond the range and interest of a home brewer. Of course, a beer that falls outside these specifications can still be a very good beer but it cannot be considered to come within that particular style.

While the home brewer can make a reasonable estimate of alcohol content by calculating from the starting and finishing gravities—and, indeed, by simply estimating from the amount of fermentables used—and can approximately measure the finished beer's colour by comparing it with a colour scale, he or she has no way of actually measuring any of these parameters. This is where a computer program like Brewers Workshop or Suds becomes invaluable, for it will calculate everything for you and enable you to plan your beer, if not with absolute accuracy then at least with enough precision to make your brewing output much more consistent and

FIGURE 14.1

This sort of sophisticated measuring equipment is not available to home brewers, but reasonable estimates can be made using home computer programs
BEHRINGER, *LÖWENBRÄU*, MUNICH 1991, P. 284

much closer to any given style than simple estimation.

For each of these recipes the parameters are stated first, then the recipe lists ingredients that should achieve something close to those figures. It should be noted, however, that these lists of ingredients are not necessarily the only way in which this profile can be achieved.

In most recipes, the base malt is described as 'pale malt', simply because the standard malt available to one home brewer will not necessary be available to the next. It is much easier and usually a good deal cheaper to use whatever malt is in plentiful supply, wherever you happen to be, rather than try to find a particular malt like a Czech pilsener malt or an English mild ale malt. If the local malt happens to be a pale ale malt, it doesn't mean you cannot brew a lager with it. When brewing a lager you should, strictly speaking, use a lager malt no more than 2L in colour (measured on the Lovibond scale), but this is not a vital consideration. Pale ale malts of around 2–5L will still brew fine lagers; it will not be possible to duplicate the very palest German and north European pilseners but anything slightly more golden, like a Munich helles or a Bohemian pilsener, will not present problems. Using a lager malt to brew ales is even less of a problem as it's easy enough to add more dark malt to get to the required colour. In fact, when brewing even pale lagers there is a fair degree of latitude as far as colour is concerned, especially as colour always appears lighter in an unfiltered beer because of the way light reflects off the tiny particles of yeast floating in it.

Unless it was considered absolutely essential for the style I have tended to avoid asking for relatively hard-to-find malts like Munich, Vienna and dextrin (Cara Pils), and I have stuck to a single type of relatively light-coloured crystal malt, 50L. If you can get only a darker style of crystal, simply use less of it, and vice versa. Most of the ingredients needed for these recipes should be available at any decent home-brew shop.

When it comes to bitterness, in some styles, like English bitter and pale ale, there is a fairly wide acceptable range because English bitters, despite their name, vary enormously in their actual bitterness level. In fact it's probably fair to say that they have varied over time as well and that current bitters tend to be less hoppy than those of 10 or 20 years ago.

Nor is it critical how you achieve that bitterness. Although tradition would say that only the finest Kent Fuggles and Goldings should be used in a pale ale, in practice, to meet a certain bitterness target you can use either a large quantity of low-alpha hops or a small amount of high-alpha varieties. It is doubtful whether any of the major British breweries still adheres strictly to using only these two varieties nowadays; they are much more likely to be using high-alpha hops for bittering and small quantities of low-alphas for aroma and flavour. The important consideration is to get the bitterness level right in terms of IBUs. For instance, if you need to hit a bitterness level of 28 IBU in a pilsener, you can do it by using 56 g (2 oz) of Hallertauer (3.5% AAU) or 24 g (just under 1 oz) of Northern Brewer (8% AAU). The difference is unlikely to be noticeable in the final flavour of the beer. In fact, many of the world's biggest brewers, and even those brewing classic styles, are achieving their ends in terms of bitterness through hop extracts and other refined hop products, not by the use of high-alpha hops, let alone 'noble' varieties.

It is important always to bear in mind that when calculating bitterness you are relying on the figures given you by your supplier. Hops may have a certain level of bitterness when harvested but by the time they reach you, that level may have dropped considerably, depending on how well the hops have been stored and handled. The importance of a supplier whose figures you can trust is vitally important if you are to achieve any reasonable degree of accuracy here.

Similarly, if the aroma or flavouring hops specified are not available, you can substitute

others. For instance, if you live in Australia or New Zealand, you are likely to have access to a good supply of fresh New Zealand and Australian hops but exotics like German Hallertauer varieties and Czech Saaz will be hard to come by and may not have travelled well. In this case it's better to use something like the excellent New Zealand Hallertauer, which may not have quite the delicacy of the original German or Czech product but is likely to be much fresher and still able to infuse good flavour and aroma into your beer. Similarly, a fine aroma hop like Willamette or Cascade would be a better choice in North America if you are not sure of the provenance of imported European hops. Naturally the effect will be different but, except for a very particular case such as a Bohemian pilsener where the original Saaz hops are a defining characteristic of the style, the result should still be within the general style. In any case, in the real world of commercial brewing, aroma is one of the areas in which beer character appears to be diminishing under market and cost pressures, so anything we do is likely to bring us closer to the original style than many commercial examples.

Hopping is usually listed as being done in three stages, the major bittering part at the start of the boil, a second addition for flavour either 10 or 15 minutes before the end and the third just as the boil is stopped in order to try for some aroma—the most difficult characteristic to achieve.

Figure 14.2

This US-bred aroma hop was released as a new variety in 1972– characterised by low bittering values, medium-strength aroma and a good yield The Hop Atlas 1994, p. 155, Joh. Barth & Sohn, Nuremberg

For details on mashing methods, see pages 80–83. I am not at all satisfied that the more complex methods of mashing produce enough benefit for the home brewer considering the amount of extra work they involve—and doing a full-mash brew is hard enough and long enough work already. However, if you have under-modified malt or you wish to try one of the more 'authentic' methods, particularly in something like a Bohemian pilsener, by all means go ahead. Sparging is an area where all sorts of complications can be introduced but again, as long as you have the sparge water at around the right temperature of 72–74°C (162–165°F) and you don't get a set sparge, small changes are unlikely to make much noticeable difference to the finished beer.

The mash recipes are based on an extract yield rate of 80 per cent; if you know that yours is lower or higher, increase or reduce the amount of base malt accordingly.

Boiling and cooling are fairly simple and fermentation depends on the style of beer being brewed and therefore the kind of yeast.

With the malt-extract recipes I have recommended the use of malto-dextrin, as it helps restore some of the body lost when the extract is condensed, plus some extra dried malt extract. You can use extract syrup if you wish but my experience is that it tends to leave a toffee-ish, cloying flavour after fermentation. Again, I have kept this fairly simple and straightforward, as malt-extract brewers usually do not want to get into needless complications. It is of course quite possible to brew malt-extract recipes without boiling the extracts, just by adding boiling water to the ingredients in the fermenter, but the technique advocated here, using a decent-sized saucepan, gives scope to add extra hops and is probably safer from a sanitation point of view.

Some styles have not been attempted because they need very special ingredients or circumstances. Among these are Belgian lambics and Berliner weisse, both of which require special yeasts and other cultures in combination, which can be tricky to work with. In particular, lambic brewing is a long process involving the use of old wooden vats, which harbour some of the yeasts and other flora essential to the style. On the other hand, although Bavarian weizen also has some unusual characteristics, most of these are due to the yeast used and that is easily obtainable, so that wheat style has been included in the recipes.

Belgian brewing is such a free-for-all that almost any recipe could be constructed within its parameters. Just one strong Belgian ale recipe has been given, approximately a Trappist dubbel, but this basic formulation can be altered by experimentation.

Most British brewers use some sort of sugar adjunct in their beers but they have had generations in which to develop expertise in blending these ingredients into their overall flavour pattern. For home brewers it is probably best to stick mainly to malt and barley adjuncts; however, if you wish to experiment with various sugars simply substitute them for an equal proportion of malt, up to a maximum of around 500 g (1 lb).

Finally, it cannot be too strongly stressed that the yeast used is of paramount importance in brewing a particular style of beer. Even the most basic of can-kit recipes will bear some resemblance to a definite style if the right yeast is used. There is a wide choice available from good home-brew stores; it's just a question of looking.

15 Packaging and serving your beer

The final stage in brewing a beer, whether commercially or in the home, is to package it ready for serving. For home brewers, that comes down to a choice between bottling and kegging. Which you choose will depend more on your on particular circumstances than on the style of beer, for most beer styles are served both ways.

If you are new to the game, then bottling is really the only choice as it requires little in the way of extra equipment over and above what you have already used for brewing. The three extras you will need are some bottles, a quantity of crown caps and some machine or device for fixing the caps on the bottles.

Bottles can be collected over the period before you start brewing or you can buy them very cheaply from a bottle bank or recycling depot. You will need either 30 of the big 750 ml bottles or 60 of the standard US 12 oz size. Crown caps can be bought anywhere you can buy a can kit. To secure the caps on the bottles the cheapest tool to use is a simple wooden baton with a metal crimping ring fitted on the end.

First, the bottles must be washed clean in hot water and dishwasher detergent, then rinsed thoroughly. Next they should be rinsed again with a mild solution of chlorine bleach, the same strength solution that you used to sanitise your fermenter (2 teaspoons to 22 litres of water). You can either rinse again after this is or just leave the bottles upside down to dry and fill them after that. (Once you have used these bottles, you should immediately rinse them out with hot water and store them upside down. Next time you will only need to rinse them again before filling.)

To give your beer the carbonation it needs to bring it to life you have to start it fermenting very briefly again. You do this by adding what is known as priming sugar before bottling it. The small amount of sugar you add will feed the yeast once more so that it will once again produce alcohol and carbon dioxide. The small amount of alcohol produced will scarcely affect the flavour or strength of the finished beer but the CO_2 will be trapped inside the sealed bottle and will dissolve into the beer, carbonating it. When the bottle is opened after two or more weeks, the beer will have a nice sparkle to it.

There are two approaches to priming. In the United States the recommended approach is to rack the beer off from the fermenter or lagering tank into another large container, add a solution of priming sugar and stir it gently in. You then bottle the beer direct from this container. Elsewhere the method used is to add a measured amount of sugar to each bottle before filling it direct from the fermenter. This saves the transferring step. US brewers claim their method results in a more even carbonation of the beer, and they are undoubtedly correct, but in many years of priming individual bottles I have yet to notice any difference between bottles that could definitely be attributed to uneven priming.

For each 750 ml bottle you will need a level teaspoonful (5 ml) of sugar, for each US 12 oz bottle, half a teaspoon. If you are bulk-priming, the figures are 150 ml for a 22.5-litre batch and $\frac{3}{4}$ cup for a US 5-gallon batch.

Whichever way you decide to prime, the next step is to transfer the beer from the fermenter or other container to the bottles. If you are using a carboy you will need to siphon it; with plastic buckets you can do it straight from the tap. Either way, you will need a length of plastic tubing of the right diameter to fit onto your tap or siphon and long enough for you to move it around from bottle to bottle as you fill. On the end of the tubing it is best to use a special bottling attachment which is fitted with a simple valve that is either spring-loaded (the best) or kept closed by the pressure of the beer. (All these items are cheaply and easily available from any good home-brew shop.) You slide the bottling tube into the bottle until the valve stem touches the bottom and is pressed open. The beer then flows into the bottle until you lift the tube and allow the valve to close. This method ensures that you can control the flow quite easily and fill all your bottles in one operation—and you get as little air into the beer as possible, thus avoiding the possibility of oxidisation, which would quickly spoil the flavour.

Before you start this you should soak the crown caps in the same kind of bleach solution you used to sanitise your fermenter. It helps if you save a litre or two of this solution each time you drain it out of the fermenter; that way you always have some to hand for little jobs like this, as well as for sanitising bottles and the equipment for culturing yeast.

Drain the crown caps, place one on top of each bottle; then, one by one, fix them on with the capping tool. Hold the capper on top of the cap and tap it firmly but gently until the cap is crimped over the bottle. Hit it too softly and it won't crimp, hit it too hard and you risk breaking the bottle, which is very messy and can be dangerous to your hands. If you don't fancy this method there are more expensive capping tools on the market that will make this part of the job virtually foolproof and a good deal quicker.

Once all the bottles are full and capped, give each a good shake to mix the priming sugar with the beer (unless you have bulk-primed), then put them away in a warm, but not too hot, place for a week or so to allow the yeast to start work on consuming the priming sugars. After that, store them in as cold place a place as you like for as long as you like. The beer should be ready to drink after two weeks but it will continue to improve slightly for some months.

Although bottling is still by far the most popular way of packaging home-brewed beer, there are other alternatives that cut out the work involved in constantly acquiring, cleaning and filling bottles.

The simplest of these is the plastic pressure barrel. This is usually a barrel-shaped container made of strong plastic to allow it to withstand pressures of up to 70 kpa (10 psi). After sanitising it in the usual away, you bulk-prime it as described above, fill it with the beer and screw the lid on tightly. After a week or two in a warm place the beer should be well carbonated. However, as you draw beer off the barrel, the pressure inside will drop and the beer will lose its carbonation. Because of this, most pressure barrels have an inlet valve which allows you to inject extra CO_2 from either sparklets-style soda siphon bulbs or a larger 5-litre (1.3-gallon) gas cylinder of the type used in home soft-drink carbonators.

Pressure barrels have some drawbacks. In the first place the internal rubber valves perish very quickly, often becoming incapable of holding enough pressure to keep the beer carbonated. The rubber can be replaced but it needs to be done frequently. In the same way, if you want to serve your beer cold and so keep the barrel in a fridge, again the rubber valves do not work very well. However, this kind of container may work very well if you are predominantly interested in serving British beers, and particularly real ale, a style in which you want neither high carbonation nor low-temperature serving.

A more practical kegging solution for home brewers is the soda keg or post-mix keg. This is a solidly built type of stainless steel keg formerly used to dispense soft drinks in pubs and bars. It comes in a variety of sizes but the most useful for our purposes are the 18-litre (US 5-gallon) and 25-litre (US 6.5-gallon) sizes. New technology has replaced the soda keg so that now there are many thousands of obsolescent kegs available at reasonable prices through home-brew shops, which often sell them equipped with the necessary fittings for attaching a CO_2 cylinder and serving the beer. Carbonation in this system is achieved by attaching the keg to a CO_2 cylinder and maintaining the required pressure with a regulator and pressure gauge. It sounds complicated but actually is quite easy to do. CO_2 cylinders can usually be hired from dealers in industrial gases and the cost is quite small. You should always take care to have the cylinder filled with food-grade CO_2.

If you have a big enough fridge, you can store one or two soda kegs in it at whatever temperature you wish and serve from them. What you do is drill one hole through the side of the fridge (taking care to avoid damaging any working parts) to allow the CO_2 line from the cylinder to go in, and another hole or two through the side or the door of the fridge to allow the beer lines out. You can even attach professional-style beer taps. You now have your own draught system and you can say goodbye to bottling forever—except perhaps for those special bocks or other strong or unusual beers that you don't want to consume too rapidly. Because the soda keg is attached to its own CO_2 supply, you do not have to prime the beer when transferring it to the keg. Just close up the keg when it is filled to the limit (which is usually the weld mark near the top of the keg) and inject the beer with gas to a pressure of around 200 kpa (30 psi). Close the gas tap after that to prevent leaks and leave the beer for about 48 hours, when it will be beautifully carbonated. This has the enormous advantage that you are transferring reasonably clear beer to the keg and do not have to go through the process of fermenting and clearing again. From time to time pressure will drop but all you have to do is turn on the gas tap every now and then, taking care not to raise the pressure in the keg to much more than 200 kpa (30 psi)—although, once your beer is carbonated, you shouldn't have to raise the pressure to much more than 70 kpa (10 psi). Obviously pubs and bars leave their draught systems with the CO_2 permanently connected and open, but to do that you have to very careful that your system does not have any leaks in it or you will lose your CO_2 to the atmosphere.

If you want to take a sample of your kegged beer to a party or dinner, there are two ways of doing it. The expensive way is to use a counter-pressure bottle-filler that will allow you to fill glass bottles without losing carbonation or pressure. The other, cheaper, way is to use a small proprietary fitting called a Carbonater, which allows you to fill PET bottles and keep them pressurised. In both cases you have the great advantage that you are bottling clear beer and you don't have to worry about how it is handled as there is no yeast sediment to disturb.

Finally, a small tip about serving beer that has been bottle-conditioned. You should always try to pour the beer in one smooth motion in order not to disturb the sediment. You can do that with a decent-sized glass and a small US 12 oz or 375 ml bottle, but if you are pouring from a 750 ml bottle you will find few glasses that will hold it all at one pour. The answer is simple—pour the beer first into a glass jug or carafe that's big enough to hold it all, and serve from there. If you take reasonable care and the yeast has settled firmly, you will always get clear beer. What more could you ask? Cheers!

16 Recipes for lagers

Bohemian pilsener

Specifications

Colour: 4–6L

Bitterness: 35–45 IBU

Original gravity:
    1.046–1.050

Alc/vol 4.5–5%

Alc/wt 3.5–4%

The characteristics of Bohemian or Czech pilsener are rich maltiness combined with a strong hop character. Smoothness is one of the hallmarks of this style so time taken in fermentation and lagering is invaluable. Either a pale ale malt or a lager malt can be used as the base malt, although the colour will be different and you may need to use a step or decoction mash for some under-modified malts. If a pale ale malt is used, the amount of crystal malt added should be reduced to about 60 g (2 oz). The hop variety used is critical in this style for it is one of the defining characteristics. Only Czech hops such as Saaz should be used throughout, for both bittering and flavour/aroma.

ALL-GRAIN

Metric (22.5 litres)		US (5 gal)
Grains/adjuncts		
4.5 kg	Pale malt	8.25 lb
100 g	Crystal malt (50L)	3.5 oz
Hops		
70 g	Saaz—full boil	2.5 oz
14 g	Saaz—10 minutes	0.4 oz
14 g	Hallertauer—end of boil	0.4 oz
Finings		
1 tsp	Irish moss	1 tsp
Yeast		
Lager yeast		

Method

Mash and sparge the grains by one of the methods described in Chapter 13. Boil the wort for 70 minutes, adding the Irish moss 30 minutes from the end the hops at intervals as directed. When cooled to below 20°C (68°F), pitch yeast. Move fermenter into modified fridge or cool area to ferment between 8 and 14°C (46–57°F) for two weeks. Bottle or keg, and lager for at least two weeks, but preferably four, at 0–3°C (32–38°F) before storing or serving. Serve at 5–7°C (41–45°F).

CAN KIT

1.8 kg	Bohemian Pilsener can kit	4 lb
750 g	Light dried malt extract	1$^1/_2$ lb
250 g	Malto-dextrin (corn syrup)	$^1/_2$ lb
14 g	Saaz hops	$^1/_2$ oz
Lager yeast		

Method

Add contents of can to at least 2 litres (2 quarts) hot water in a large saucepan. Bring to the boil, stirring constantly to prevent sticking and burning, add dried extract and malto-dextrin, then simmer for 10 minutes. Switch off heat then add the Saaz hops and stir. Leave for 2 minutes then strain into fermenter and top up with cold water plus ice if necessary. When cooled to below 20°C (68°F), pitch yeast. Move fermenter into modified fridge or cool area to ferment between 8g and 14°C (46–57°F) for two weeks. Bottle or keg, and lager for at least two weeks, but preferably four, at 0–3°C (32–38°F) before storing or serving. Serve at 5–7°C (41–45°F).

German pilsener

German pilsener is a paler and lighter style than the Czech original so we are aiming to produce a pale golden beer in which the malt flavour is largely dominated by the hops. Smoothness is one of the hallmarks of this style so time taken in fermentation and lagering is invaluable. Either a pale ale malt or a lager malt can be used, although the colour will be different and you may need to use a step or decoction mash for some under-modified malts. Almost any kind of hops cane be used for bittering, but aroma hops should be used for at least the final addition. It should be noted that some German brewers hop in only one stage, so that is also an option.

Specifications

Colour: 3–6 L
Bitterness: 30–40 IBU
Original gravity:
   1.046–1.050
Alc/vol 4.5–5%
Alc/wt 3.5–4%

ALL-GRAIN

Metric (22.5 litres)		US (5 gal)
Grains/adjuncts		
4.5 kg	Pale malt	8.25 lb
Hops		
32 g	Northern Brewer—full boil	0.9 oz
14 g	Willamette—10 minutes	0.4 oz
14 g	Willamette—end of boil	0.4 oz
Finings		
1 tsp	Irish moss	1 tsp
Yeast		
Lager yeast.		

Method

Mash and sparge the grains by one of the methods described in Chapter 13. Boil the wort for 70 minutes, adding the Irish moss 30 minutes from the end and hops at intervals as directed. When cooled to below 20°C (68°F), pitch yeast. Move fermenter into modified fridge or cool area to ferment between 8–14°C (46–57°F) for two weeks. Bottle or keg, and lager for at least two weeks, but preferably four, at 0–3°C (32–38°F) before storing or serving. Serve at 5–7°C (41–45°F).

CAN KIT

1.8 kg	Pilsner lager can kit	4 lb
500 g	Light dried malt extract	1 lb
500 g	Malto-dextrin (corn syrup)	1 lb
14 g	Willamette hops	$^{1}/_{2}$ oz
Lager yeast		

Method

Add contents of can to at least 2 litres (2 quarts) hot water in a large saucepan. Bring to the boil stirring constantly to prevent sticking and burning, add dried extract and malto-dextrin then simmer for 10 minutes. Switch off heat then add the Willamette hops and stir. Leave for 2 minutes then strain into fermenter and top up with cold water plus ice if necessary. When cooled to below 20°C (68°F), pitch yeast. Move fermenter into modified fridge or cool area to ferment between 8–14°C (46–57°F) for two weeks. Bottle or keg, and lager for at least two weeks, but preferably four, at 0–3°C (32–38°F) before storing or serving. Serve at 5–7°C (41–45°F).

North European pilsener

Specifications

Colour: 3–4L

Bitterness: 22–24 IBU

Original gravity:
  1.046–1.050

Alc/vol 4.5–5%

Alc/wt 3.5–4%

The difference between German and other north European pilseners is slight, and relates mainly to the body of the beer and the degree of hop bitterness. North European pilseners tend to be crisp and refreshing with the hop element relatively understated. Adjuncts may or may not be used, depending on the brewer, and lagering times need not be as long as for the more malty versions of the style. Either a pale ale malt or a lager malt can be used, although a lager malt is preferable for the pale colour required. The variety of hops used for bittering is relatively unimportant as long as the final bitterness figure is within the specified range. Aroma hops are preferable for at least the final addition, although the hopping can be done in one stage if necessary, in which case the two later hopping steps are omitted. The New Zealand Hallertauer hops used in this recipe are a rare combination of high-alpha (10 AAU) and aroma.

ALL-GRAIN

Metric (22.5 litres)		US (5 gal)
Grains/adjuncts		
4 kg	Pale malt	7.25 lb
500 g	Flaked maize	1 lb
Hops		
14 g	NZ Hallertauer—full boil	0.4 oz
14 g	NZ Hallertauer—15 minutes	0.4 oz
14 g	NZ Hallertauer—end of boil	0.4 oz
Finings		
1 tsp	Irish moss	1 tsp
Yeast		
Lager yeast		

Method

Mash and sparge the grains by one of the methods described in Chapter 13. Boil the wort for 70 minutes, adding Irish moss 30 minutes from the end and the hops at intervals as directed. When cooled to below 20°C (68°F), pitch yeast. Move fermenter into modified fridge or cool area to ferment between 8 and 14°C (46–57°F) for two weeks. Bottle or keg, and lager for at least two weeks, but preferably four, at 0–3°C (32–38°F) before storing or serving. Serve at 5–7°C (41–45°F).

CAN KIT

1.8 kg	Dutch lager can kit	4 lb
500 g	Light dried malt extract	1 lb
500 g	Malto-dextrin (corn syrup)	1 lb
14 g	Aroma hops (optional)	1/2 oz
Lager yeast		

Method

Add contents of can to at least 2 litres (2 quarts) hot water in a large saucepan. Bring to the boil stirring constantly to prevent sticking and burning, add dried extract and malto-dextrin, then simmer for 10 minutes. Switch off heat, then add the aroma hops and stir. Leave for 2 minutes then strain into fermenter and top up with cold water plus ice if necessary. When cooled to below 20°C (68°F), pitch yeast. Move fermenter into modified fridge or cool area to ferment between 8 and 14°C (46–57°F) for two weeks. Bottle or keg, and lager for at least two weeks, but preferably four, at 0–3°C (32–38°F) before storing or serving. Serve at 5–7°C (41–45°F).

Munich helles

Specifications
Colour: 3–6L
Bitterness: 18–25 IBU
Original gravity:
    1.046–1.052
Alc/vol 4.5–5%
Alc/wt 3.5–4%

Munich helles is one of the two great pale lager styles. It is in many ways similar to a pilsener, but whereas a pilsener is almost a display case for the hops, a helles accentuates malt flavours. Smoothness is one of the hallmarks of this style, so time taken in fermentation and lagering is invaluable. Fermentation should take around two weeks and lagering, at around 0°C (32°F), at least four weeks, to develop the genuine helles liquid gold palate. Either a pale ale malt or a lager malt can be used as the base malt, although the colour will be different and you may need to use a step or decoction mash for some under-modified malts. The hop varieties used for bittering are not critical, but it is essential to use only fine aroma hops for the later additions.

ALL-GRAIN

Metric (22.5 litres)		US (5 gal)
Grains/adjuncts		
4.5 kg	Pale malt	8.25 lb
Hops		
46 g	Hallertauer—full boil	1.4 oz
14 g	Hallertauer—10 minutes	0.4 oz
14 g	Hallertauer—end of boil	0.4 oz
Finings		
1 tsp	Irish moss	1 tsp
Yeast		
Lager yeast		

Method

Mash and sparge the grains by one of the methods described in Chapter 13. Boil the wort for 70 minutes, adding the Irish moss 30 minutes from the end and the hops at intervals as directed. When cooled to below 20°C (68°F), pitch yeast. Move fermenter into modified fridge or cool area to ferment between 8 and 14°C (46–57°F) for two weeks. Bottle or keg, and lager for at least two weeks, but preferably four, at 0–3°C (32–38°F) before storing or serving. Serve at 5–7°C (41–45°F).

CAN KIT

1.8 kg	Munich helles can kit	4 lb
500 g	Light dried malt extract	1 lb
500 g	Malto-dextrin (corn syrup)	1 lb
14 g	Aroma hops	1/2 oz
Lager yeast		

Method

Add contents of can to at least 2 litres (2 quarts) hot water in a large saucepan. Bring to the boil, stirring constantly to prevent sticking and burning, add dried extract and malto-dextrin, then simmer for 10 minutes. Switch off heat, then add the aroma hops and stir. Leave for 2 minutes, then strain into fermenter and top up with cold water plus ice if necessary. When cooled to below 20°C (68°F), pitch yeast. Move fermenter into modified fridge or cool area to ferment between 8 and 14°C (46–57°F) for two weeks. Bottle or keg, and lager for at least two weeks at 0–3°C (32–38°F) before storing or serving. Serve at 5–7°C (41–45°F).

Dortmunder export

Perhaps reflecting the fact that Dortmund is and was an important trading city which has always sold its beer all over Germany as well as overseas, Dortmunder beers tend to be easy-drinking styles with a smooth balance between malt and hops that slightly favours the malt. They are not quite as malty as Munich's helles nor as hoppy as a pilsener, but somewhere in between. This actually makes it a relatively simple matter to brew in this style, assuming you are familiar with basic lager technique. Fermentation is conducted at around 10°C (50°F) and lagering should be for at least two weeks. Either a pale ale malt or a lager malt can be used, for Dortmund beers vary a little in colour from the lightish DAB (Dortmunder Actien Brauerei) to the slightly darker Kronen. Hops are not critical as long as the final bitterness figure is within the specified range. Aroma hops should be used for at least the final addition if at all possible.

Specifications
Colour: 3–6L
Bitterness: 24–29 IBU
Original gravity:
    1.048–1.055
Alc/vol 5–5.5%
Alc/wt 4–4.5%

ALL-GRAIN

Metric (22.5 litres)		US (5 gal)
Grains/adjuncts		
5 kg	Pale malt	9 lb
Hops		
30 g	Cascade—full boil	1 oz
14 g	Cascade—10 minutes	0.4 oz
14 g	Cascade—end of boil	0.4 oz
Finings		
1 tsp	Irish moss	1 tsp
Yeast		
Lager yeast		

Method

Mash and sparge the grains by one of the methods described in Chapter 13. Boil the wort for 70 minutes, adding the Irish moss 30 minutes from the end and the hops at intervals as directed. When cooled to below 20°C (68°F), pitch yeast. Move fermenter into modified fridge or cool area to ferment between 8 and 14°C (46–57°F) for two weeks. Bottle or keg, and lager for at least two weeks, but preferably four, at 0–3°C (32–38°F) before storing or serving. Serve at 5–7°C (41–45°F).

CAN KIT

1.8 kg	Dortmunder export can kit	4 lb
500 g	Light dried malt extract	1 lb
500 g	Malto-dextrin (corn syrup)	1 lb
14 g	Aroma hops	1/2 oz
Lager yeast		

Method

Add contents of can to at least 2 litres (2 quarts) hot water in a large saucepan. Bring to the boil, stirring constantly to prevent sticking and burning, add dried extract and malto-dextrin, then simmer for 10 minutes. Switch off heat, then add the aroma hops and stir. Leave for 2 minutes, then strain into fermenter and top up with cold water plus ice if necessary. When cooled to below 20°C (68°F), pitch yeast. Move fermenter into modified fridge or cool area to ferment between 8 and 14°C (46–57°F) for two weeks. Bottle or keg, and lager for at least two weeks at 0–3°C (32–38°F) before storing or serving. Serve at 5–7°C (41–45°F).

Vienna

Specifications
Colour: 8–12L
Bitterness: 22–27 IBU
Original gravity:
    1.048–1.056
Alc/vol 5– 5.5%
Alc/wt 4–4.5%

Vienna lager is, or was, closely related to the oktoberfest/märzen style. The problem is that it is no longer brewed in the city where it was created and is only kept alive by revivalist breweries in other parts of the world, so there is no longer a classic standard by which to judge it. However, we can take it to be a tawny lager, not quite as strong as the festival beers but with a palate just as skewed towards maltiness, once again balanced by firm hopping with high-quality aroma hops. As with the festival beers, lagering is important to stabilise and mature the beer. It should be fermented at around 10°C (50°F), and lagered for at least four weeks. Lager malt is preferable to pale malt for these tawny lagers, but pale ale malt can be used if that's all you can get hold of, supplemented with crystal to heighten colour and dextrin malt to give extra body. Traditionally, high-quality Bavarian hops are used, and the bitterness level must be reasonably high to balance out the large amounts of malt used. However, while it is quite acceptable to use high-alpha hops for the bittering, for the later hop additions, aroma hops like Hallertauer, Tetttnang, Hersbrücker and Saaz are advisable.

ALL-GRAIN

Metric (22.5 litres)		US (5 gal)
Grains/adjuncts		
4 kg	Pale malt	7.25 lb
250 g	Crystal 50	7.5 oz
500 g	Dextrin malt	15 oz
Hops		
30 g	Hallertauer—full boil	1 oz
14 g	Hallertauer—10 minutes	0.4 oz
14 g	Saaz—end of boil	0.4 oz
Finings		
1 tsp	Irish moss	1 tsp
Yeast		
Lager yeast		

Method

Mash and sparge the grains by one of the methods described in Chapter 13. Boil the wort for 70 minutes, adding the Irish moss 30 minutes from the end and the hops at intervals as directed. When cooled to below 20°C (68°F), pitch yeast. Move fermenter into modified fridge or cool area to ferment between 8–14°C (46–57°F) for two weeks. Bottle or keg, and lager for at least two weeks, but preferably four, at 0–3°C (32–38°F) before storing or serving. Serve at 5–7°C (41–45°F).

CAN KIT

1.8 kg	Vienna lager can kit	4 lb
500 g	Light dried malt extract	1 lb
500 g	Malto-dextrin (corn syrup)	1 lb
14 g	Aroma hops	1/2 oz
Lager yeast		

Method

Add contents of can to at least 2 litres (2 quarts) hot water in a large saucepan. Bring to the boil, stirring constantly to prevent sticking and burning, add dried extract and malto-dextrin, then simmer for 10 minutes. Switch off heat, then add the aroma hops and stir. Leave for 2 minutes, then strain into fermenter and top up with cold water plus ice if necessary. When cooled to below 20°C (68°F), pitch yeast. Move fermenter into modified fridge or cool area to ferment between 8 and 14°C (46–57°F) for two weeks. Bottle or keg, and lager for at least two weeks at 0–3°C (32–38°F) before storing or serving. Serve at 5–7°C (41–45°F).

Bavarian dunkel 1

Specifications

Colour: 16–22L

Bitterness: 15–25 IBU

Original gravity:
   1.050–1.055

Alc/vol 5–5.5%

Alc/wt 4–4.4%

In one sense, dark beers are easier to brew than pale ones because the strong flavours of the dark malts help to cover up any deficiencies in brewing technique or any slight infections that may have crept in. On the other hand, and for the very same reason, it can be difficult to express an individual character in a dark beer without resorting to gimmicks. German brewers are not allowed gimmicks, so a dunkel lager has to be a careful blend of malt and hops, and it has to be thoroughly attenuated to avoid a cloying taste of malty sweetness. The variety of hops used for bittering is relatively unimportant as long as the final bitterness figure is within the specified range. Although the Bavarian brewers would have originally used aroma hops from the Hallertau, aroma hops are not an important feature of the style these days, and late hopping can be omitted. A strong-acting lager yeast that will fully attenuate the brew is essential.

ALL-GRAIN

Metric (22.5 litres)		US (5 gal)
Grains/adjuncts		
5 kg	Munich malt	9 lb
200 g	Crystal malt 50L	7 oz
100 g	Black patent malt	3.5 oz
Hops		
40 g	Hallertauer—full boil	1.5 oz
14 g	Hallertauer—15 minutes	0.4 oz
14 g	Hallertauer—end of boil	0.4 oz
Finings		
1 tsp	Irish moss	1 tsp
Yeast		
Lager yeast		

Method

Mash and sparge the grains by one of the methods described in Chapter 13. Boil the wort for 70 minutes, adding Irish moss 30 minutes from the end, and the hops at intervals as directed. When cooled to below 20°C (68°F), pitch yeast. Move fermenter into modified fridge or cool area to ferment between 8 and 14°C (46–57°F) for two weeks. Bottle or keg, and lager for at least two weeks, but preferably four, at 0–3°C (32–38°F) before storing or serving. Serve at 5–7°C (41–45°F).

CAN KIT

1.8 kg	Munich dark lager can kit	4 lb
500 g	Amber/dark dried malt extract	1 lb
500 g	Malto-dextrin (corn syrup)	1 lb
14 g	Aroma hops (optional)	$^1/_2$ oz
Lager yeast		

Method

Add contents of can to at least 2 litres (2 quarts) hot water in a large saucepan. Bring to the boil, stirring constantly to prevent sticking and burning, add dried extract and malto-dextrin, then simmer for 10 minutes. Switch off heat, then add the aroma hops and stir. Leave for 2 minutes, then strain into fermenter and top up with cold water plus ice if necessary. When cooled to below 20°C (68°F), pitch yeast. Move fermenter into modified fridge or cool area to ferment between 8 and 14°C (46–57°F) for two weeks. Bottle or keg, and lager for at least two weeks, but preferably four, at 0–3°C (32–38°F) before storing or serving. Serve at 5–7°C (41–45°F).

Bavarian dunkel 2

Although Munich malt is the preferred base malt for Bavarian dark lagers, it is not always readily available—and if you are accustomed to buying your malt cheaply in bulk, you are unlikely to want to have 50 kg (110 lbs) of Munich malt lying around your home brewery waiting to be used up. The alternative is to use your standard pale malt and extra dark malts. The hopping and other steps are exactly the same.

Specifications
Colour: 16–22L
Bitterness: 15–25 IBU
Original gravity:
    1.050–1.055
Alc/vol 5–5.5%
Alc/wt 4–4.4%

ALL-GRAIN

Metric (22.5 litres)		US (5 gal)
Grains/adjuncts		
5 kg	Pale malt	9 lb
200 g	Crystal malt 50L	7 oz
100 g	Black patent malt	3.5 oz
Hops		
40 g	Hallertauer—full boil	1.5 oz
14 g	Hallertauer—15 minutes	0.4 oz
14 g	Hallertauer—end of boil	0.4 oz
Finings		
1 tsp	Irish Moss	1 tsp
Yeast		
Lager yeast		

Method

Mash and sparge the grains by one of the methods described in Chapter 13. Boil the wort for 70 minutes, adding Irish moss 30 minutes from the end, and the hops at intervals as directed. When cooled to below 20°C (68°F), pitch yeast. Move fermenter into modified fridge or cool area to ferment between 8 and14°C (46–57°F) for two weeks. Bottle or keg, and lager for at least two weeks, but preferably four, at 0–3°C (32–38°F) before storing or serving. Serve at 5–7°C (41–45°F).

CAN KIT

1.8 kg	Munich dark lager can kit	4 lb
500 g	Amber dried malt extract	1 lb
500 g	Malto-dextrin (corn syrup)	1 lb
14 g	Aroma hops (optional)	$^{1}/_{2}$ oz
Lager yeast		

Method

Add contents of can to at least 2 litres (2 quarts) hot water in a large saucepan. Bring to the boil, stirring constantly to prevent sticking and burning, add dried extract and malto-dextrin, then simmer for 10 minutes. Switch off heat, then add the aroma hops and stir. Leave 2 minutes, then strain into fermenter and top up with cold water plus ice if necessary. When cooled to below 20°C (68°F), pitch yeast. Move fermenter into modified fridge or cool area to ferment between 8 and 14°C (46–57°F) for two weeks. Bottle or keg, and lager for at least two weeks at 0–3°C (32–38°F) before storing or serving. Serve at 5–7°C (41–45°F).

Oktoberfest/Märzen

Specifications

Colour: 4–16L
Bitterness: 22–28 IBU
Original gravity:
   1.052–1.065
Alc/vol 5.5–6%
Alc/wt 4.5–5%

Oktoberfest and märzen are the same beer by two different names. The name 'oktoberfest' comes from the fact that the beer was brewed to be drunk at the great Oktoberfest festival, while märzen comes from the German word for March, which is when the beer was actually brewed. Between times it was stored in the Bavarian caves to mature. Its colour varies quite considerably, but it is essentially a tawny lager with a strongly malty palate balanced by firm hopping with high-quality aroma hops. In view of its history, lagering is obviously particularly important for this style, thus after fermentation for around two weeks it should be lagered for at least four weeks, and longer if possible. Lager malt is preferable to pale malt for these tawny lagers, but pale ale malt can be used if that's all you can get hold of, supplemented with crystal to heighten colour and dextrin malt to give extra body. Traditionally, high-quality Bavarian hops are used and the bitterness level must be reasonably high to balance out the large amounts of malt. However, it is quite acceptable to use high-alpha hops for the bittering. For the later hop additions, aroma hops like Hallertauer,

Tetttnang, Hersbrücker and Saaz are advisable.

ALL-GRAIN

Metric (22.5 litres)		US (5 gal)
Grains/adjuncts		
4.5 kg	Pale malt	8.25 lb
400 g	Crystal 50	12 oz
500 g	Dextrin malt	15 oz
Hops		
54 g	Hallertauer—full boil	1.6 oz
14 g	Hallertauer—10 minutes	0.4 oz
14 g	Saaz—end of boil	0.4 oz
Finings		
1 tsp	Irish moss	1 tsp
Yeast		
Lager yeast		

Method

Mash and sparge the grains by one of the methods described in Chapter 13. Boil the wort for 70 minutes, adding the Irish moss 30 minutes from the end, and the hops at intervals as directed. When cooled to below 20°C (68°F), pitch yeast. Move fermenter into modified fridge or cool area to ferment between 8 and 14°C (46–57°F) for two weeks. Bottle or keg, and lager for at least two weeks, but preferably four, at 0–3°C (32–38°F) before storing or serving. Serve at 5–7°C (41–45°F).

CAN KIT

1.8 kg	Oktoberfest/märzen can kit	4 lb
750 g	Light dried malt extract	1.4 lb
500 g	Malto-dextrin (corn syrup)	1 lb
14 g	Aroma hops	$^1/_2$ oz
Lager yeast		

Method

Add contents of can to at least 2 litres (2 quarts) hot water in a large saucepan. Bring to the boil, stirring constantly to prevent sticking and burning, add dried extract and malto-dextrin, then simmer for 10 minutes. Switch off heat, then add the aroma hops and stir. Leave for for 2 minutes, then strain into fermenter and top up with cold water plus ice if necessary. When cooled to below 20°C (68°F), pitch yeast. Move fermenter into modified fridge or cool area to ferment between 8 and 14°C (46–57°F) for two weeks. Bottle or keg, and lager for at least two weeks at 0–3°C (32–38°F) before storing or serving. Serve at 5–7°C (41–45°F).

Helles bock

Specifications

Colour: 6–8L

Bitterness: 22–28 IBU

Original gravity:
   1.064–1.070

Alc/vol 6.4–6.8%

Alc/wt 5.2–5.6%

Despite the popular myths about home-brewed beer blowing your head off, the fact is that strong beers are the most difficult to brew at home. In fact, one of the reasons for the myth is that, in attempting to make strong beer, too many people have simply added extra sugar and the result has been an evil potion fit only to create the mother and father of all hangovers. A bock is a beautifully crafted beer that takes time and care to brew and mature. The type of malt used depends very much on whether you are brewing a pale helles bock or a dark dunkel bock. Because big mashes become difficult to handle in a home-brewing situation, this recipe uses some dried malt extract to bring the gravity up into the required range. Although the malt dominates the flavour of a bock, the hops are still important to keep it in balance and prevent cloying. Fine aroma hops should be used for bittering and aroma/flavour.

ALL-GRAIN

Metric (22.5 litres)		US (5 gal)
3 kg	Pale malt	5.5 lb
2 kg	Munich malt	3.5 lb
1 kg	Light dried malt extract	2 lb
60 g	Hallertauer—full boil	1.8 oz
30 g	Hallertauer—10 minutes	1 oz
14 g	Hallertauer—end of boil	0.4 oz
1 tsp	Irish moss	1 tsp
Lager yeast		

Method

Mash and sparge the grains by one of the methods described in Chapter 13. Boil the wort for 70 minutes, adding the Irish moss 30 minutes from the end, and the hops at intervals as directed. Add the dried extract 10 minutes from the end. When cooled to below 20°C (68°F), pitch yeast. Move fermenter into modified fridge or cool area to ferment between 8 and 14°C (46–57°F) for two weeks. Bottle or keg, and lager for at least four weeks, but preferably eight, at 0–3°C (32–38°F) before storing or serving. Serve at 5–7°C (41–45°F).

CAN KIT

1.8 kg	Bock can kit	4 lb
1 kg	Light dried malt extract	2 lb
500 g	Malto-dextrin (corn syrup)	1 lb
14 g	Aroma hops (optional)	$^1/_2$ oz
Lager yeast		

Method

Add contents of can, extract and malto-dextrin to at least 3 litres (3 quarts) hot water in a large saucepan. Bring to the boil, stirring constantly to prevent sticking and burning, then simmer for 10 minutes. Switch off heat, then add the aroma hops and stir. Leave 2 minutes, then strain into fermenter and top up with cold water plus ice if necessary. When cooled to below 20°C (68°F), pitch yeast. Move fermenter into modified fridge or cool area to ferment between 8–14°C (46–57°F) for two weeks. Bottle or keg, and lager for at least four weeks at 0–3°C (32–38°F) before storing or serving. Serve at 5–7°C (41–45°F).

American/Canadian light

The biggest selling beer in the world is Anheuser-Busch's Budweiser, and it sets the standard for what has to be considered one of the important world beer styles simply by virtue of its popularity. American beers of this type put a premium on being crisp and refreshing. Hop character is prominent in the aroma and flavour of the beer but bitterness is very low by world, and particularly German, standards. Adjuncts are commonly used; 'Bud' is famous for the use of rice as a body-lightener but other brands tend to use more corn (maize) adjuncts. Fermentation temperatures should still be low but not necessarily below 10°C (50°F), and lagering times are short, from a week to 10 days. A lager malt must be used in order to get the necessary lightness. The variety of hops used for bittering is relatively unimportant as long as the final bitterness figure is within the specified range. Aroma hops are preferable for at least the final addition. It may surprise some to be told that Anheuser-Busch are heavy users of high-quality aroma hops, although the floral character evident in the nose should make that clear.

Specifications

Colour: 2–4L
Bitterness: 22–24 IBU
Original gravity:
    1.046–1.050
Alc/vol 4.5–5%
Alc/wt 3.5–4%

ALL-GRAIN

Metric (22.5 litres)		US (5 gal)
Grains/adjuncts		
4 kg	Pale malt	7.25 lb
500 g	Flaked rice	1 lb
Hops		
14 g	Cascade—full boil	0.4 oz
14 g	Cascade—10 minutes	0.4 oz
14 g	Willamette	0.4 oz
Finings		
1 tsp	Irish moss	1 tsp
Yeast		
Lager yeast		

Method

Mash and sparge the grains by one of the methods described in Chapter 13. Boil the wort for 70 minutes, adding Irish moss 30 minutes from the end, and the hops at intervals as directed. When cooled to below 20°C (68°F), pitch yeast. Move fermenter into modified fridge or cool area to ferment between 8 and 14°C (46–57°F) for two weeks. Bottle or keg, and lager for at least two weeks, but preferably four, at 0–3°C (32–38°F) before storing or serving. Serve at 5–7°C (41–45°F).

CAN KIT

1.8 kg	American lager can kit	4 lb
500 g	Light dried malt extract	1 lb
500 g	Rice malt syrup	1 lb
14 g	Aroma hops (optional)	$1/2$ oz
Lager yeast		

Method

Add contents of can to at least 2 litres (2 quarts) hot water in a large saucepan. Bring to the boil, stirring constantly to prevent sticking and burning, add dried extract and rice malt syrup, then simmer for 10 minutes. Switch off heat, then add the aroma hops and stir. Leave for 2 minutes, then strain into fermenter and top up with cold water plus ice if necessary. When cooled to below 20°C (68°F), pitch yeast. Move fermenter into modified fridge or cool area to ferment between 8 and 14°C (46–57°F) for two weeks. Bottle or keg, and lager for at least two weeks at 0–3°C (32–38°F) before storing or serving. Serve at 5–7°C (41–45°F).

American premium

Specifications

Colour: 12–16L

Bitterness: 24–26 IBU

Original gravity:
   1.052

Alc/vol 4.75%

Alc/wt 3.8%

With the introduction of Samuel Adams Boston Lager, the Boston Beer Company created, virtually overnight, a new style of beer that for these purposes we can call an American premium lager. In style it is actually close to a vienna or märzen, though it is a normal-strength beer. Like those German/Austrian styles it is a tawny-to-dark lager with a strongly malty palate balanced by firm hopping with high-quality aroma hops. In the case of Samuel Adams, the hop character is taken almost as far as it can go without becoming unbalanced. It is not especially bitter (except when judged by US standards) but the hop aroma and flavour are conspicuous and lasting. Normal lager fermentation and lagering practices should be followed—fermentation for about two weeks, then lagering for another four. As this beer is so close in some respects to a pale ale, pale ale malt can be used if necessary plus the necessary dark malts. High-quality Bavarian and Czech hops are essential to approximate this style. The company has published specifications from which the figures below are taken but, as we are brewing this as a style rather than a copy, they need not be followed slavishly. In any case, original gravity will vary depending on your mash set-up.

ALL-GRAIN

Metric (22.5 litres)		US (5 gal)
Grains/adjuncts		
5k g	Pale malt	9 lb
200 g	Crystal 50	7 oz
50 g	Chocolate malt	1.5 oz
Hops		
42 g	Hallertauer Mittelfrüh—full boil	1.5 oz
14 g	Hallertauer Mittelfrüh—10 minutes	0.5 oz
30 g	Tettnang-dry hopped	1 oz
Finings		
1 tsp	Irish moss	1 tsp
Yeast		
Lager yeast		

Method

Mash and sparge the grains by one of the methods described in Chapter 13. Boil the wort for 70 minutes, adding the Irish moss 30 minutes from the end, and the hops at intervals as directed. When cooled to below 20°C (68°F), pitch yeast. Move fermenter into modified fridge or cool area to ferment between 8 and 14°C (46–57°F) for two weeks. At the end of the first week, add the dry Tettnang hops. Bottle or keg, and lager for at least two weeks, but preferably four, at 0–3°C (32–38°F) before storing or serving. Serve at 5–7°C (41–45°F).

CAN KIT

1.8 kg	Oktoberfest/märzen/vienna can kit	4 lb
500 g	Light dried malt extract	1 lb
500 g	Malto-dextrin (corn syrup)	1 lb
14 g	Aroma hops	$1/2$ oz
30 g	Aroma hops—dry hopped	1 oz
Lager yeast		

Method

Add contents of can to at least 2 litres (2 quarts) hot water in a large saucepan. Bring to the boil, stirring constantly to prevent sticking and burning, add dried extract and malto-dextrin, then simmer for 10 minutes. Switch off heat, then add the aroma hops and stir. Leave for 2 minutes, then strain into fermenter and top up with cold water plus ice if necessary. When cooled to below 20°C (68°F), pitch yeast. Move fermenter into modified fridge or cool area to ferment between 8 and 14°C (46–57°F) for two weeks. At the end of the first week add the dry hops. Bottle or keg, and lager for at least two weeks at 0–3°C (32–38°F) before storing or serving. Serve at 5–7°C (41–45°F).

Australian standard

Specifications
Colour: 2–4L
Bitterness: 16–20 IBU
Original gravity:
    1.045–1052
Alc/vol 4.5–5.5%
Alc/wt 4–4.5%

The defining characteristics of Australian lagers are the use of cane sugar adjuncts and high-alpha Pride of Ringwood hops, often in the form of pre-isomerised extracts that do not have to be boiled but can be added straight to the brew. However, the effects of these practices on the flavour of a beer are not easily realised in a home-brewing situation. In fact, using corn sugar in the form of powdered dextrose probably gives us a closer approximation of the Australian style than simply adding cane sugar, which tends to give a syrupy, almost Belgian, accent to the beer. Late hopping is not a characteristic of this style and it is essential to use Pride of Ringwood hops. Australian beers have no sulphur undertones so a classic European lager yeast is unlikely to produce a beer in this style. Something like Wyeast's versatile California Lager Yeast, fermented at around 15°C (60°F), should get fairly close.

ALL-GRAIN

Metric (22.5 litres)		US (5 gal)
Grains/adjuncts		
4.5 kg	Pale malt	8.25 lb
500 g	Dextrose (in boil)	15 oz
Hops		
20 g	Pride of Ringwood	0.6 oz
Finings		
1 tsp	Irish moss	1 tsp
Yeast		
Lager yeast (see above)		

Method

Mash and sparge the grains by one of the methods described in Chapter 13. Boil the wort for 70 minutes, adding the dextrose and all the hops at the start, and the Irish moss 30 minutes from the end. When cooled to below 20°C (68°F) pitch yeast. Ferment at around 15°C (60°F) for one week. Bottle or keg, and lager for at least two weeks at 0–3°C (32–38°F) before storing or serving. Serve at 5–7°C (41–45°F).

CAN KIT

1.8 kg	Australian lager can kit	4 lb
250 g	Light dried malt extract	$1/2$ lb
250 g	Malto-dextrin (corn syrup)	$1/2$ lb
500 g	Dextrose	1 lb
Lager yeast		

Method

Add contents of can to at least 2 litres (2 quarts) hot water in a large saucepan. Bring to the boil, stirring constantly to prevent sticking and burning, add dried extract, dextrose and malto-dextrin, then simmer for 10 minutes. Strain into fermenter and top up with cold water plus ice if necessary. When cooled to below 20°C (68°F), pitch yeast. Move fermenter into modified fridge or cool area to ferment between 8 and 14°C (46–57°F) for two weeks. Bottle or keg, and lager for at least two weeks at 0–3°C (32–38°F) before storing or serving. Serve at 5–7°C (41–45°F).

New Zealand premium

New Zealanders grow hops with huge alpha-acid counts yet their beer is characteristically mild-finishing. Cynics might say this indicates a desire to keep hopping costs down but in the case of New Zealand's most successful beer export, Steinlager, the process has produced a pleasant and very drinkable pilsener-style lager. Cane sugar adjuncts are less obvious in this style but the lightness of body indicates that some sort of non-malt product is being used. Late hopping can be done with New Zealand hops such as their Hallertauer triploid, which has excellent aroma characteristics as well as high alphas (10%). A normal lager yeast should be used at temperatures of around 10–14°C (50–57°F). Specifications are very similar to an Australian lager but the flavour and aroma are quite different.

Specifications

Colour: 2–4L

Bitterness: 18–24 IBU

Original gravity: 1.045–1052

Alc/vol 4.5–5.5%

Alc/wt 4–4.5%

ALL-GRAIN

Metric (22.5 litres)		US (5 gal)
Grains/adjuncts		
4.5 kg	Pale malt	8.25 lb
250 g	Flaked rice	7.5 oz
Hops		
14 g	NZ Hallertauer—start of boil	0.4 oz
14 g	NZ Hallertauer—15 minutes	0.4 oz
14 g	NZ Hallertauer—end of boil	0.4 oz
Finings		
1 tsp	Irish moss	1 tsp
Yeast		
Lager yeast (see above)		

Method

Mash and sparge the grains by one of the methods described in Chapter 13. Boil the wort for 70 minutes, adding the hops at intervals as directed, and the Irish moss 30 minutes from the end. When cooled to below 20°C (68°F), pitch yeast. Ferment at around 15°C (59°F) for one week. Bottle or keg, and lager for at least two weeks at 0–3°C (32–38°F) before storing or serving. Serve at 5–7°C (41–45°F).

CAN KIT

1.8 kg	Australian lager can kit	4 lb
250 g	Light dried malt extract	$^1/_2$ lb
750 g	Malto-dextrin (corn syrup)	$1^1/_2$ lb
14 g	NZ Hallertauer hop pellets	$^1/_2$ oz
Lager yeast		

Method

Add contents of can to at least 2 litres (2 quarts) hot water in a large saucepan. Bring to the boil, stirring constantly to prevent sticking and burning, add dried extract and malto-dextrin, then simmer for 10 minutes. Switch off heat, then add the hop pellets and stir. Leave for 2 minutes, then strain into fermenter and top up with cold water plus ice if necessary. When cooled to below 20°C (68°F), pitch yeast. Move fermenter into modified fridge or cool area to ferment between 8 and 14°C (46–57°F) for two weeks. Bottle or keg, and lager for at least two weeks at 0–3°C (32–38°F) before storing or serving. Serve at 5–7°C (41–45°F).

17 Recipes for ales

English pale bitter

Specifications

Colour: 6–12L

Bitterness: 22–34 IBU

Original gravity:
1.035–1.040

Alc/vol 3.5–4%

Alc/wt 3–3.5%

Bitters come in all shades and hues, from almost the pale gold of a lager to the rich chocolate of a porter. They are probably the easiest of beers to brew in the home situation because their top-fermentation works well at room temperatures and is very quick. Bitters are not usually stored for long periods so freshness is a desirable characteristic. For brewers, this means a bitter can be ready for drinking within not much more than 10 days of starting to brew. It will not necessarily be completely clear, but that is not a major consideration. Either a pale ale malt or a lager malt can be used as the base malt, although the colour will be different. The hop variety used is not critical, particularly for bittering, but to get a real bitter character, you should try to use classic Kent hops like Goldings or Fuggles for flavour and aroma.

ALL-GRAIN

Metric (22.5 litres)		US (5 gal)
Grains/adjuncts		
3 kg	Pale malt	6.5 lb
500 g	Flaked barley	15 oz
200 g	Crystal malt (50L)	6 oz
Hops		
50 g	Goldings—full boil	1.5 oz
14 g	Goldings—10 minutes	0.4 oz
14 g	Goldings—end of boil	0.4 oz
Finings		
1 tsp	Irish moss	1 tsp
Yeast		
Ale yeast		

Method

Mash and sparge the grains by one of the methods described in Chapter 13. Boil the wort for 70 minutes, adding the Irish moss 30 minutes from the end, and the hops at intervals as directed. When cooled to below 20°C (68°F), pitch yeast. Ferment between 16 and 21°C (60–70°F) for two weeks. Bottle or keg. Serve at 8–12°C (45–55°F).

1.8 kg	English bitter can kit	4 lb
500 g	Light dried malt extract	1 lb
500 g	Malto-dextrin (corn syrup)	1 lb
14 g	Goldings hop pellets	$^1/_2$ oz
Ale yeast		

Method

Add contents of can to at least 2 litres (2 quarts) hot water in a large saucepan. Bring to the boil, stirring constantly to prevent sticking and burning, add dried extract, malto-dextrin and hop pellets, then simmer for 10 minutes. Pour into fermenter and top up with cold water plus ice if necessary. When temperature is below 25°C (77°F), pitch yeast. Ferment between 16 and 21°C for one to two weeks. Serve at 8–12°C (45–55°F).

English dark bitter

Specifications

Colour: 10–18L

Bitterness: 20–28 IBU

Original gravity:
  1.035–1.040

Alc/vol 3.5–4%

Alc/wt 3–3.5%

The darker style of English bitter hovers somewhere between the mild and brown ale styles, stronger than a mild but not as strong as a brown, but definitely more bitter than either. However, a late hop aroma and flavour are not necessarily part of this style, which takes its main characteristic from the dark malts used in the mash. Again, this is a relatively quick and easy beer to brew and one in which you can use almost any hop for bittering. Either a pale ale malt or a lager malt can be used as the base malt, although the colour will be different. If a pale ale malt is used, the amount of crystal malt added should be reduced a little.

ALL-GRAIN

Metric (22.5 litres)		US (5 gal)
Grains/adjuncts		
3.5 kg	Pale malt	6.5 lb
400 g	Crystal malt (50L)	12 oz
50 g	Chocolate malt	1.5 oz
Hops		
26 g	Northern Brewer—full boil	1 oz
Finings		
1 tsp	Irish moss	1 tsp
Yeast		
Ale yeast		

Method

Mash and sparge the grains by one of the methods described in Chapter 13. Boil the wort for 70 minutes, adding the hops and the Irish moss 30 minutes from the end. When cooled to below 20°C (68°F), pitch yeast. Ferment between 16–21°C (60–70°F) for one to two weeks. Serve at 8–12°C (45–55°F).

CAN KIT

1.8 kg	English dark bitter can kit	4 lb
500 g	Light dried malt extract	1 lb
500 g	Malto-dextrin (corn syrup)	1 lb
14 g	Fuggles hop pellets	$^{1}/_{2}$ oz
Ale yeast		

Method

Add contents of can to at least 2 litres (2 quarts) hot water in a large saucepan. Bring to the boil, stirring constantly to prevent sticking and burning, add dried extract, malto-dextrin and hop pellets, then simmer for 10 minutes. Pour into fermenter and top up with cold water plus ice if necessary. When cooled to below 25°C (77°F) pitch yeast. Ferment between 16 and 21°C for one to two weeks. Serve at 8–12°C (45–55°F).

Special bitter

The next step up the alcohol ladder from ordinary bitter, special bitter is simply a little more of the same—more malt, more hops—though there is plenty of room for variation, as can be seen from the commercial examples available. Colour is usually a light brown. Again, this style is not usually stored for long periods, so freshness is a desirable characteristic, even though its extra strength gives it better keeping prospects and usually means a little longer wait before drinking. Whereas an ordinary bitter can be ready for drinking within around 10 days of starting to brew, a special bitter should wait for at least two weeks, and a little longer will do no harm. Either a pale ale malt or a lager malt can be used as the base malt, although the colour will be different. The hop variety used for bittering is not critical, but for character there is nothing to beat the traditional Kent varieties.

Specifications

Colour: 8–14L
Bitterness: 30–46 IBU
Original gravity:
  1.040–1.045
Alc/vol 4–4.5%
Alc/wt 3.2–3.6%

ALL-GRAIN

Metric (22.5 litres)		US (5 gal)
Grains/adjuncts		
4 kg	Pale malt	7.5 lb
200 g	Crystal malt (50L)	6 oz
50 g	Chocolate malt	1.5 oz
Hops		
75 g	Fuggles—full boil	2.25 oz
14 g	Fuggles—10 minutes	0.4 oz
14 g	Goldings—at end	0.4 oz
Finings		
1 tsp	Irish moss	1 tsp
Yeast		
Ale yeast		

Method

Mash and sparge the grains by one of the methods described in Chapter 13. Boil the wort for 70 minutes, adding the Irish moss 30 minutes from the end, and the hops at intervals as directed. When cooled to below 20°C (68°F), pitch yeast. Ferment between 16–21°C (60–70°F) for two weeks. Bottle or keg. Serve at 8–12°C (45–55°F).

CAN KIT

1.8 kg	Brown ale can kit	4 lb
500 g	Light dried malt extract	1 lb
500 g	Malto-dextrin (corn syrup)	1 lb
14 g	Goldings hop pellets	$^1/_2$ oz
Ale yeast		

Method

Add contents of can to at least 2 litres (2 quarts) hot water in a large saucepan. Bring to the boil, stirring constantly to prevent sticking and burning, add dried extract, malto-dextrin and hop pellets, then simmer for 10 minutes. Pour into fermenter and top up with cold water plus ice if necessary. When cooled to below 25°C (77°F), pitch yeast. Ferment between 16 and 21°C for one to two weeks. Serve at 8–12°C (45–55°F).

Extra special bitter

This is the aristocrat of the world of bitters—a beer that tips the balance of the style towards the malty side without losing the strong hoppiness that its name implies. If special bitter is a 'little more of the same', extra special bitter is about as far as you can go without getting into strong ale territory. Colour is again usually a light brown, though smaller quantities of the dark malts are used, the rest of the colour coming from the increased amount of base malt. Freshness is not so important here and an extra special bitter will not be ready for drinking for around a month after starting to brew—and longer will do no harm. Either a pale ale malt or a lager malt can be used as the base malt, although the colour will be different. The hop variety used for bittering is not critical, but for character there is nothing to beat the traditional Kent varieties, Goldings in particular.

Specifications

Colour: 8–14L
Bitterness: 30–46 IBU
Original gravity:
  1.045–1.060
Alc/vol 4.5–6%
Alc/wt 3.6–4.8%

ALL-GRAIN

Metric (22.5 litres)		US (5 gal)
Grains/adjuncts		
4.5 kg	Pale malt	7.5 lb
100 g	Crystal malt (50L)	3 oz
50 g	Chocolate malt	1.5 oz
Hops		
70 g	Goldings—full boil	2 oz
14 g	Goldings—10 minutes	0.4 oz
14 g	Goldings—at end	0.4 oz
Finings		
1 tsp	Irish moss	1 tsp
Yeast		
Ale yeast		

Method

Mash and sparge the grains by one of the methods described in Chapter 13. Boil the wort for 70 minutes, adding the Irish moss 30 minutes from the end, and the hops at intervals as directed. When cooled to below 20°C (68°F), pitch yeast. Ferment between 16 and 21°C (60–70°F) for at least four weeks, longer if possible. Bottle or keg. Serve at 8–12°C (45–55°F).

CAN KIT

1.8 kg	Extra special bitter can kit	4 lb
750 g	Light dried malt extract	1.5 lb
500 g	Malto-dextrin (corn syrup)	1 lb
14 g	Goldings hop pellets	$^1/_2$ oz
Ale yeast		

Method

Add contents of can to at least 2 litres (2 quarts) hot water in a large saucepan. Bring to the boil, stirring constantly to prevent sticking and burning, add dried extract, malto-dextrin and hop pellets, then simmer for 10 minutes. Pour into fermenter and top up with cold water plus ice if necessary. When cooled to below 25°C (77°F), pitch yeast. Ferment between 16 and 21°C for one to two weeks. Serve at 8–12°C (45–55°F).

Brown ale

Specifications

Colour: 15–24L

Bitterness: 16–22 IBU

Original gravity:
　1.040–1.050

Alc/vol 4–5%

Alc/wt 3.2–4%

The name tells the story. The aim in brewing this style is to produce a beer that is distinctly brown in colour and we do that by using dark malts along with the base malt. Brown ales are usually a little stronger than ordinary bitters, but not as strongly hopped, and the finish is relatively sweet. Like bitters, brown ales are not usually stored for long periods so freshness is a desirable characteristic. However, brown ales are more likely than bitters to be bottled, so keeping them in storage for a while is not at all out of character. Thus a brown ale can be ready for drinking within not much more than 10 days of starting to brew, but will also keep for months. Either a pale ale malt or a lager malt can be used as the base malt, although the colour will be different. The hop variety used is not critical, particularly for bittering, and hop flavour and aroma are usually subservient to the dark malt character.

ALL-GRAIN

Metric (22.5 litres)		US (5 gal)
Grains/adjuncts		
4 kg	Pale malt	7 lb
300 g	Crystal malt (50L)	9 oz
150 g	Chocolate malt	4.5 oz
Hops		
22 g	Northern Brewer—full boil	0.7 oz
14 g	Fuggles—10 minutes	0.4 oz
Finings		
1 tsp	Irish moss	1 tsp
Yeast		
Ale yeast		

Method

Mash and sparge the grains by one of the methods described in Chapter 13. Boil the wort for 70 minutes, adding the Irish moss 30 minutes from the end, and the hops at intervals as directed. When cooled to below 20°C (68°F), pitch yeast. Ferment between 16 and 21°C (60–70°F) for two weeks. Bottle or keg. Serve at 8–12°C (45–55°F).

CAN KIT

1.8 kg	Brown ale can kit	4 lb
500 g	Light dried malt extract	1 lb
500 g	Malto-dextrin (corn syrup)	1 lb
14 g	Fuggles hop pellets	1/2 oz
Ale yeast		

Method

Add contents of can to at least 2 litres (2 quarts) hot water in a large saucepan. Bring to the boil, stirring constantly to prevent sticking and burning, add dried extract, malto-dextrin and hop pellets, then simmer for 10 minutes. Pour into fermenter and top up with cold water plus ice if necessary. When cooled to below 25°C (77°F), pitch yeast. Ferment between 16 and 21°C for one to two weeks. Serve at 8–12°C (45–55°F).

English mild

Mild may have lost some of its natural market to lager, a beer at the opposite end of the colour spectrum, but it is still a very pleasant style to drink and quite easy to brew. Milds are not necessarily low in alcohol, as the mildness suggested by the name really refers to the degree of bitterness. This is another style in which a late hop aroma and flavour are not necessary, as the dark malts used in the mash define the richly malty nature of the style. Colour varies enormously as the specification indicates, and the darkest examples are quite close to pale porters. Again this is a relatively quick and easy beer to brew and one in which you can use almost any hop for bittering. Either a pale ale malt or a lager malt can be used as the base malt, although the colour will be different. If a pale ale malt is used, the amount of crystal malt added should be reduced a little.

Specifications

Colour: 10–30L
Bitterness: 20–28 IBU
Original gravity:
    1.030–1.038
Alc/vol 3.5–4%
Alc/wt 3–3.5%

ALL-GRAIN

Metric (22.5 litres)		US (5 gal)
Grains/adjuncts		
3.0 kg	Pale malt	5.5 lb
500 g	Crystal malt (50L)	15 oz
200 g	Black patent malt	6 oz
Hops		
30 g	Fuggles—full boil	1 oz
Finings		
1 tsp	Irish moss	1 tsp
Yeast		
Ale yeast		

Method

Mash and sparge the grains by one of the methods described in Chapter 13. Boil the wort with the hops for 70 minutes, adding the Irish moss 30 minutes from the end. When cooled to below 20°C (68°F), pitch yeast. Ferment between 16 and 21°C (60–70°F) for two weeks. Bottle or keg. Serve at 8–12°C (45–55°F).

CAN KIT

1.8 kg	English dark bitter can kit	4 lb
500 g	Light dried malt extract	1 lb
500 g	Malto-dextrin (corn syrup)	1 lb
14 g	Fuggles hop pellets	$^1/_2$ oz
Ale yeast		

Method

Add contents of can to at least 2 litres (2 quarts) hot water in a large saucepan. Bring to the boil, stirring constantly to prevent sticking and burning, add dried extract, malto-dextrin and hop pellets, then simmer for 10 minutes. Pour into fermenter and top up with cold water plus ice if necessary. When cooled to below 25°C (77°F), pitch yeast. Ferment between 16 and 21°C for one to two weeks. Serve at 8–12°C (45–55°F).

Old ale

Specifications

Colour: 16–24L
Bitterness: 24–36 IBU
Original gravity:
  1.050–1.060
Alc/vol: 5–6%;
Alc/wt: 4–4.8%

The designation 'old ale' is usually given to dark, strongish beers, probably because the style predates the use of pale malts. Old ales in the English sense are often richly flavoured and not usually highly hopped. However, there is wide variation among commercial examples and they can be very strong indeed—verging on barley wine territory. This recipe is not a very strong brew. It uses a very small amount of molasses to give the unusual, wine-like effect typical of the famous Old Peculier brewed by Theakston's in Yorkshire. Ideally a pale ale malt should be used as the base malt, but a lager malt will also fit the bill. Hopping is not high and hop flavour and aroma are restrained, so the hop variety used is not critical—although a low-alpha variety will tend to give more character.

ALL-GRAIN

Metric (22.5 litres)		US (5 gal)
Grains/adjuncts		
4 kg	Pale malt	6$^1/_2$ lb
500 g	Flaked barley	15 oz
500 g	Crystal malt (50L)	15 oz
100 g	Black malt	3 oz
50 g	Molasses	1$^1/_2$ oz
Hops		
30 g	Northern brewer—full boil	0.9 oz
14 g	Fuggles—10 mins	0.4 oz
Finings		
1 tsp (5 ml)	Irish moss	1 tsp
Yeast		
Ale yeast		

Method

Mash and sparge the grains by one of the methods described in Chapter 13. Boil the wort for 70 minutes, adding the Irish moss 30 minutes from the end, and the hops at intervals as directed. When cooled to below 20°C (68°F), pitch yeast. Ferment at 16–21°C (60–70°F) for two weeks. Bottle or keg. Serve at 8–12°C (45–55°F).

CAN KIT

1.8 kg	Old ale can kit	4 lb
500 g	Dark dried malt extract	1 lb
500 g	Malto-dextrin (corn syrup)	1 lb
50 g	Molasses	1^1/$_2$ oz
14 g	Fuggles hop pellets	^{1}/$_2$ oz
Ale yeast		

Method

Add contents of can to at least 2 litres (2 quarts) of hot water in a large saucepan. Bring to the boil (stirring constantly to prevent sticking and burning), add dried extract, molasses, malto-dextrin and hop pellets, and then simmer for 10 minutes. Pour into fermenter and top up with cold water (plus ice if necessary). When temperature is below 25°C (77°F), pitch yeast. Ferment at 16–21°C for one to two weeks. Serve at 8–12°C (45–55°F).

Irish red ale

Irish red is a style that has become widely known because of the mushrooming growth of 'Irish Pubs' all over the world. Falling somewhere between a Scottish heavy and an English brown ale, its distinguishing features are its brick-red colouring and its smooth, creamy head. The head is obtained by pressurising the beer in the keg with nitrogen, which forms smaller bubbles in the beer than carbon dioxide and also doesn't dissolve so readily into it, so the beer is not highly carbonated. Although it is possible for home brewers to use nitrogen, or a CO_2/nitrogen mix, in their keg systems, this is not really convenient unless you are going to be kegging only this kind of beer and Guinness-style stout. The other characteristics, however, can be easily achieved by using the right proportions of different malts. Ideally a pale ale malt should be used as the base malt but a lager malt will also fit the bill. Hopping is not high, and hop flavour and aroma are restrained, so the hop variety used is not critical, although a low-alpha variety will tend to give more character.

Specifications

Colour: 16–24L
Bitterness: 20–24 IBU
Original gravity:
   1.040–1.050
Alc/vol 4–5%
Alc/wt 3.2–4%

ALL-GRAIN

Metric (22.5 litres)		US (5 gal)
Grains/adjuncts		
3.5 kg	Pale malt	6.5 lb
500 g	Crystal malt (50L)	15 oz
50 g	Chocolate malt	1.5 oz
Hops		
40 g	Fuggles—full boil	1.2 oz
14 g	Fuggles—10 minutes	0.4 oz
Finings		
1 tsp	Irish moss	1 tsp
Yeast		
Ale yeast		

Method

Mash and sparge the grains by one of the methods described in Chapter 13. Boil the wort for 70 minutes, adding the Irish moss 30 minutes from the end, and the hops at intervals as directed. When cooled to below 20°C (68°F), pitch yeast. Ferment between 16 and 21°C (60–70°F) for two weeks. Bottle or keg. Serve at 8–12°C (45–55°F).

CAN KIT

1.8 kg	Irish Ale can kit	4 lb
500 g	Light dried malt extract	1 lb
500 g	Malto-dextrin (corn syrup)	1 lb
14 g	Fuggles hop pellets	1/2 oz
Ale yeast		

Method

Add contents of can to at least 2 litres (2 quarts) hot water in a large saucepan. Bring to the boil, stirring constantly to prevent sticking and burning, add dried extract, malto-dextrin and hop pellets, then simmer for 10 minutes. Pour into fermenter and top up with cold water plus ice if necessary. When cooled to below 25°C (77°F), pitch yeast. Ferment between 16 and 21°C for one to two weeks. Serve at 8–12°C (45–55°F).

Scottish heavy

Specifications

Colour: 10–20L

Bitterness: 14–22 IBU

Original gravity:
  1.036–1.042

Alc/vol 3.6–4.2%

Alc/wt 2.8–3.4%

Where the English describe their two basic beers as mild or bitter, north of the border the terminology is light or heavy—or it used to be until some bright young thing decided to revive the old designations of Scottish ales by the mythical shilling value of the cask. Thus heavy is a 70/- ale, and so on (see pages 44–5). The old designations seem to me to be easier and neater, so that's what we will use here. Perhaps one of the reasons for the different nomenclature was that Scottish heavies tended never to be very bitter anyway, leaning more to the malty side and closely related to the English brown ale. However, small Scottish revivalist breweries are now putting definitely more of a hop character into their beers than before, so the malt–hops balance is shifting slightly. Otherwise this is a straightforward brownish beer, brewed in the same way as any other British ale. This is another beer that can be consumed very fresh and can be ready for drinking within around 10 days of starting to brew.

ALL-GRAIN

Metric (22.5 litres)		US (5 gal)
Grains/adjuncts		
3.25 kg	Pale malt	6 lb
250 g	Crystal malt	7.5 oz
50 g	Black malt	1.5 oz
Hops		
30 g	Fuggles—full boil	0.9 oz
14 g	Fuggles—15 mins	0.4 oz
14 g	Fuggles—at end	0.4 oz
Finings		
1 tsp	Irish moss	1 tsp
Yeast		
Ale yeast		

Method
Mash and sparge the grains by one of the methods described in Chapter 13. Boil the wort for 70 minutes, adding the Irish moss 30 minutes from the end, and the hops at intervals as directed. When cooled to below 20°C (68°F), pitch yeast. Ferment between 16 and 21°C (60–70°F) for two weeks. Bottle or keg. Serve at 8–12°C (45–55°F).

CAN KIT

1.8 kg	Stout can kit	4 lb
500 g	Light dried malt extract	1 lb
500 g	Malto-dextrin (corn syrup)	1 lb
14 g	Fuggles hop pellets	1/2 oz
Ale yeast		

Method
Add contents of can to at least 2 litres (2 quarts) hot water in a large saucepan. Bring to the boil, stirring constantly to prevent sticking and burning, add dried extract, malto-dextrin and hop pellets, then simmer for 10 minutes. Pour into fermenter and top up with cold water plus ice if necessary. When temperature is below 25°C (77°F), pitch yeast. Ferment between 16 and 21°C for one to two weeks. Serve at 8–12°C (45–55°F).

Scottish light

Specifications

Colour: 14–24L

Bitterness: 10–20 IBU

Original gravity:
1.030–1.036

Alc/vol 3–3.5%

Alc/wt 2.4–2.8%

The principal differences between Scottish lights and heavies are alcoholic strength and colour. The hopping is at similar levels, though light seldom exhibits any strong hop aroma of flavour, probably because it simply isn't strong enough to carry it. This is a darkish, very straightforward beer to brew. It may seem to be a little lacking in ingredients but the dark malts and the mild hopping should combine to produce a refreshing and tasty drop. Again, this is a beer that can be consumed very fresh and can be ready for drinking within 10 days of starting to brew.

ALL-GRAIN

Metric (22.5 litres)		US (5 gal)
Grains/adjuncts		
2.7 kg	Pale malt	5 lb
400 g	Crystal malt	12 oz
100 g	Chocolate malt	3 oz
Hops		
30 g	Fuggles—full boil	0.9 oz
Finings		
1 tsp	Irish moss	1 tsp
Yeast		
Ale yeast		

Method

Mash and sparge the grains by one of the methods described in Chapter 13. Boil the wort for 70 minutes, adding the Irish moss 30 minutes from the end. When cooled to below 20°C (68°F), pitch yeast. Ferment between 16 and 21°C (60–70°F) for two weeks. Bottle or keg. Serve at 8–12°C (45–55°F).

CAN KIT

1.8 kg	Scottish light can kit	4 lb
500 g	Light dried malt extract	1 lb
250 g	Malto-dextrin (corn syrup)	8oz
14 g	Fuggles hop pellets	1/2 oz
Ale yeast		

Method

Add contents of can to at least 2 litres (2 quarts) hot water in a large saucepan. Bring to the boil, stirring constantly to prevent sticking and burning, add dried extract, hop pellets and malto-dextrin, then simmer for 10 minutes. Pour into fermenter and top up with cold water plus ice if necessary. When cooled to below 25°C (77°F), pitch yeast. Ferment between 16 and 21°C for one to two weeks. Serve at 8–12°C (45–55°F).

Pale ale

Pale ale and bitter are almost interchangeable styles. The only real difference is that pale ale is more restricted in its colour range. As the name implies, there can be no dark pale ale—although the actual colour is hardly pale by comparison with a pilsener. It earned the designation 'pale' by comparison with the dark beers like porter and mild, with which it was competing. Pale ale is usually towards the stronger end of the bitters spectrum, somewhere around the level of extra special bitter; and it should always be highly hopped, preferably with classic Kent varieties like Fuggles and Goldings, although high-alpha varieties can be used for bittering. While bitters are not usually stored for long periods, pale ales, being originally a bottled style, can handle a little more maturing and are therefore good for bottling. The strongest type of pale ale, India Pale Ale, was originally brewed with export in mind so freshness is not so important a characteristic. Ideally a pale ale malt should be used as the base malt, but a lager malt will also fit the bill.

Specifications

Colour: 4–12L
Bitterness: 22–40 IBU
Original gravity:
   1.045–1.055
Alc/vol 4.5–5.5%
   Alc/wt 3.6–4.4%

ALL-GRAIN

Metric (22.5 litres)		US (5 gal)
Grains/adjuncts		
4.5 kg	Pale malt	8.25 lb
100 g	Crystal malt (50L)	3 oz
Hops		
60 g	Fuggles—full boil	1.8 oz
14 g	Goldings—10 minutes	0.4 oz
14 g	Goldings—end of boil	0.4 oz
Finings		
1 tsp	Irish moss	1 tsp
Yeast		
Ale yeast		

Method
Mash and sparge the grains by one of the methods described in Chapter 13. Boil the wort for 70 minutes, adding the Irish moss 30 minutes from the end, and the hops at intervals as directed. When cooled to below 20°C (68°F), pitch yeast. Ferment between 16–21°C (60–70°F) for two weeks. Bottle or keg. Serve at 8–12°C (45–55°F).

CAN KIT

1.8 kg	Pale ale can kit	4 lb
500 g	Light dried malt extract	1 lb
500 g	Malto-dextrin (corn syrup)	1 lb
14 g	Goldings hop pellets	1/2 oz
Ale yeast		

Method
Add contents of can to at least 2 litres (2 quarts) hot water in a large saucepan. Bring to the boil, stirring constantly to prevent sticking and burning, add dried extract, malto-dextrin and hop pellets, then simmer for 10 minutes. Pour into fermenter and top up with cold water plus ice if necessary. When temperature is below 25°C (77°F), pitch yeast. Ferment between 16–21°C for one to two weeks. Serve at 8–12°C (45–55°F).

Porter

Specifications
Colour: 20–69L
Bitterness: 20–40 IBU
Original gravity:
    1.040–1.060
Alc/vol 4–6%
Alc/wt 3.2–4.8%

The main problem when formulating a recipe for porter is that no one knows exactly what it should be. The style died out in the first quarter of the twentieth century and, although it has been revived, the exact composition of the original beer has been lost forever. Given, however, that porter's heyday was in the era before exact measurements were possible in brewing, it's safe to assume that recipes would have varied considerably from brew to brew, so we have plenty of room for manoeuvre. Certainly it was, and is, a very dark beer, while not quite as dark as stout, but how it got its colour is the cause of some dispute. It may well have been brewed from a dark base malt, though current practice with traditional dark lagers in Bavaria indicates that, in its later stages, some brewers may have used pale base malts together with roasted malts. In any case, most of us have little alternative but to follow this course, as dark base malts are not always easy to find. This is a dry, fairly highly hopped style, but the hops are there almost entirely for bitterness as the dark malts dominate the flavour. Any good hops variety can be used for bittering, while aroma is not necessarily a feature of the style. This is another beer that can be consumed very fresh and can be ready for drinking within around 10 days of starting to brew.

ALL-GRAIN

Metric (22.5 litres)		**US (5 gal)**
Grains/adjuncts		
4.5 kg	Pale malt	8.25 lb
500 g	Crystal malt (50L)	15 oz
300 g	Chocolate malt	9 oz
Hops		
30 g	Northern Brewer—full boil	0.9 oz
Finings		
1 tsp	Irish moss	1 tsp
Yeast		
Ale yeast		

Method

Mash and sparge the grains by one of the methods described in Chapter 13. Boil the wort for 70 minutes, adding the Irish moss 30 minutes from the end. When cooled to below 20°C (68°F), pitch yeast. Ferment between 16–21°C (60–70°F) for two weeks. Bottle or keg. Serve at 8–12°C (45–55°F).

CAN KIT

1.8 kg	Porter can kit	4 lb
500 g	Amber dried malt extract	1 lb
500 g	Malto-dextrin (corn syrup)	1 lb
14 g	Northern Brewer hop pellets	$^1/_2$ oz
Ale yeast		

Method

Add contents of can to at least 2 litres (2 quarts) hot water in a large saucepan. Bring to the boil, stirring constantly to prevent sticking and burning, add dried extract, malto-dextrin and hop pellets, then simmer for 10 minutes. Pour into fermenter and top up with cold water plus ice if necessary. When cooled to below 25°C (77°F), pitch yeast. Ferment between 16 and 21°C for one to two weeks. Serve at 8–12°C (45–55°F).

Stout

Stout appears to be a style derived from porter, but the offspring has proved sturdier in the long run, or perhaps just more fitted for survival in the modern world, than its parent. It seems that stronger styles of porter might have been called 'stout porter', using the word 'stout' in its earlier meaning to indicate strength rather than roundness, and that the second part of the name dropped off in common usage—as did the word 'ale' in 'bitter ale'. In any case, stout is as dark as a beer gets. There are two styles, dry and sweet, but the dry is by far the more common, to the extent that sweet stout is almost a threatened species. The style has given birth to perhaps the best-known beer name in the world, Guinness, and stout is brewed all over the world, from Britain to the United States, India to Australia. It has become the national drink of Ireland. This is a dry, fairly highly hopped style, but the hops are there almost entirely for bitterness as the dark malts dominate the flavour. Any good variety can be used for bittering, while aroma is not a feature of the style. This is another beer that can be consumed very fresh and can be ready for drinking within around 10 days of starting to brew. This recipe will not produce the darkest possible stout but it is a good place to start. You can add further dark malts if you prefer a really black brew.

Specifications

Colour: 40–70L

Bitterness: 30–40 IBU

Original gravity:
  1.040–1.060

Alc/vol 4–6%

Alc/wt 3.2–4.8%

ALL-GRAIN

Metric (22.5 litres)		US (5 gal)
Grains/adjuncts		
4 kg	Pale malt	7.5 lb
500 g	Flaked barley	15 oz
500 g	Roast barley	15 oz
Hops		
30 g	Bullion—full boil	0.9 oz
Finings		
1 tsp	Irish moss	1 tsp
Yeast		
Ale yeast		

Method

Mash and sparge the grains by one of the methods. When cooled to below 20°C (68°F), pitch yeast. Ferment between 16 and 21°C (60–70°F) for two weeks. Bottle or keg. Serve at 8–12°C (45–55°F).

CAN KIT

1.8 kg	Stout can kit	4 lb
750 g	Dark dried malt extract	1.5 lb
500 g	Malto-dextrin (corn syrup)	1 lb
14 g	Bullion hop pellets	1/2 oz
Ale yeast		

Method

Add contents of can to at least 2 litres (2 quarts) hot water in a large saucepan. Bring to the boil, stirring constantly to prevent sticking and burning, add dried extract, malto-dextrin and hop pellets, then simmer for 10 minutes. Pour into fermenter and top up with cold water plus ice if necessary. When cooled to below 25°C (77°F), pitch yeast. Ferment between 16 and 21°C for one to two weeks. Serve at 8–12°C (45–55°F).

Australian sparkling

Specifications

Colour: 4–8L

Bitterness: 24–30 IBU

Original gravity:
1.050–1.060

Alc/vol 5–6%

Alc/wt 4–5%

Although Australia is predominantly a lager-drinking country, a few ales are still brewed there. The sparkling ale style was developed by one of the last major family-owned breweries in the country, Thomas Cooper's, and despite its name, its most notable characteristic is its cloudiness, as it is one of the very few beers in the country that is bottle-conditioned. Each bottle gets a dose of fresh yeast as it is filled, which makes the beer a very good source of fresh yeast for the home brewer. In fact, if you really want to replicate this style of beer you need either to culture this yeast from the bottle or to buy a commercial liquid yeast under the name of 'Australian ale yeast'—which is very likely the same yeast. The most important property of Cooper's yeast is that it ferments strongly and truly to quite high temperatures, up to and over 25°C (77°F), without creating too many odd flavours. It also gives a light fruit character to the beer. Pride of Ringwood hops are the standard variety used, but other high-alpha varieties can be substituted. Since Cooper's is one of the few brewers selling can kits under their own name, you can use one of their kits as a base for the extract brew.

ALL-GRAIN

Metric (22.5 litres)		US (5 gal)
Grains/adjuncts		
4.5 kg	Pale malt	7.8 lb
100 g	Crystal malt	3 oz
500 g	White sugar	15 oz
Hops		
28 g	Pride of Ringwood—full boil	0.9 oz
Finings		
1 tsp	Irish moss	1 tsp
Yeast		
Australian ale yeast		

Method
Mash and sparge the grains by one of the methods described in Chapter 13. Boil the wort for 70 minutes, adding the Irish moss 30 minutes from the end. When cooled to below 20°C (68°F), pitch yeast. Ferment between 16 and 18°C (60–64°F) for one to two weeks. Bottle or keg, and leave for at least two weeks before serving. Serve at 6–8°C (42–46°F).

CAN KIT

1.8 kg	Coopers Draught can kit	4 lb
500 g	Light dried malt extract	1 lb
250 g	Malto-dextrin (corn syrup)	1/2 lb
250 g	White sugar	1/2 lb
14 g	Pride of Ringwood hop pellets	1/2 oz
Australian ale yeast		

Method
Add contents of can to at least 2 litres (2 quarts) hot water in a large saucepan. Bring to the boil, stirring constantly to prevent sticking and burning, add dried extract, white sugar, malto-dextrin and hop pellets, then simmer for 10 minutes. Pour into fermenter and top up with cold water plus ice if necessary. When cooled to below 25°C (77°F), pitch yeast. Ferment between 16 and 18°C (60–64°F) for one to two weeks. Bottle or keg and store for at least two weeks before serving. Serve at 6–8°C (42–46°F).

Kölsch

Specifications

Colour: 3–6L

Bitterness: 22–32 IBU

Original gravity:
    1.042–1.046

Alc/vol 4.5–4.8%

Alc/wt 3.6–3.8%

The beer of Cologne (Köln) is one of the most precise and well-defined styles in the world. It is a pale, top-fermented beer of around average strength with firm hopping and good, natural carbonation. It could be considered the ale world's answer to a pilsener, as it has a similar colour, if perhaps a little darker, and distinct sulphur notes on the nose and palate, particularly when it warms up. This is no doubt one of the reasons it is served in small glasses—so that it will not have time to get too warm. Hopping rates are in the middle range and hop flavour and aroma are pronounced, so it is important only to use the best German hops, at least for the flavour and aroma stages. Kölsch yeasts have been evolved to produce the necessary characteristics for this style so if you want to get close to it you should follow suit. A British-style ale yeast will produce a pleasant beer, but not the real thing.

ALL-GRAIN

Metric (22.5 litres)		**US (5 gal)**
Grains/adjuncts		
4.5 kg	Pale malt	8.25 lb
Hops		
46 g	Tettnanger—full boil	1.4 oz
14 g	Tettnanger—10 minutes	0.4 oz
14 g	Tettnanger—at end	0.4 oz
Finings		
1 tsp	Irish moss	1 tsp
Yeast		
Kölsch or other ale yeast		

Method

Mash and sparge the grains by one of the methods described in Chapter 13. Boil the wort for 70 minutes, adding the Irish moss 30 minutes from the end, and the hops at intervals as directed. When cooled to below 20°C (68°F) pitch yeast. Ferment between 16 and 18°C (60–64°F) for one to two weeks. Bottle or keg and store for at least two weeks before serving. Serve at 6–8°C (42–46°F).

CAN KIT

1.8 kg	Kölsch can kit	4 lb
500 g	Light dried malt extract	1 lb
500 g	Malto-dextrin (corn syrup)	1 lb
14 g	Fuggles hop pellets	1/2 oz
Kölsch or other yeast		

Method

Add contents of can to at least 2 litres (2 quarts) hot water in a large saucepan. Bring to the boil, stirring constantly to prevent sticking and burning, add dried extract, molasses, malto-dextrin and hop pellets, then simmer for 10 minutes. Pour into fermenter and top up with cold water plus ice if necessary. When cooled to below 25°C (77°F), pitch yeast. Ferment between 16 and 18°C (60–64°F) for one to two weeks. Bottle or keg and store for at least two weeks before serving. Serve at 6–8°C (42–46°F).

Altbier

The word *alt* in German simply means 'old', and altbier is a style similar to the beers that were brewed throughout Germany before the discovery of bottom-fermentation. The centre of alt brewing is Düsseldorf, where it is the dominant style, but as alt is not a style delineated by an *appellation controlée* it is also brewed in other parts of Germany. As brewed in Düsseldorf, alt is a dark, top-fermented beer of around average strength with firm hopping and good natural carbonation. It is the closest that German beer gets to a British style, but lacks the fruitiness of most British beers. Alt is made either with a dark base malt, like a Munich malt, or with a pale pilsener-style malt to which is added various dark malts to get the characteristic chocolate colour. Hopping rates are in the middle range but hop flavour and aroma are not pronounced, so the variety of hops used is relatively unimportant. Special alt yeasts are available and should be used if you want to get really close to the original style, but any good, strongly attenuating ale yeast should do the job quite well.

Specifications

Colour: 12–20L
Bitterness: 26–46 IBU
Original gravity:
   1.042–1.046
Alc/vol 4.5–4.8%
Alc/wt 3.6–3.8%

ALL-GRAIN

Metric (22.5 litres)		US (5 gal)
Grains/adjuncts		
4.25 kg	Pale malt	7.8 lb
300 g	Crystal malt	9 oz
100 g	Chocolate malt	3 oz
Hops		
30 g	Northern Brewer—full boil	0.9 oz
14 g	Hallertauer—10 minutes	0.4 oz
Finings		
1 tsp	Irish moss	1 tsp
Yeast		
Altbier or other ale yeast		

Method

Mash and sparge the grains by one of the methods described in Chapter 13. Boil the wort for 70 minutes, adding the Irish moss 30 minutes from the end, and the hops at intervals as directed. When cooled to below 20°C (68°F), pitch yeast. Ferment between 16–18°C (60–64°F) for one to two weeks. Bottle or keg and leave for at least two weeks before serving. Serve at 6–8°C (42–46°F).

CAN KIT

1.8 kg	Altbier can kit	4 lb
500 g	Amber dried malt extract	1 lb
500 g	Malto-dextrin (corn syrup)	1 lb
14 g	Northern Brewer hop pellets	$^1/_2$ oz
Altbier or other ale yeast		

Method

Add contents of can to at least 2 litres (2 quarts) hot water in a large saucepan. Bring to the boil, stirring constantly to prevent sticking and burning, add dried extract, malto-dextrin and hop pellets, then simmer for 10 minutes. Pour into fermenter and top up with cold water plus ice if necessary. When cooled to below 25°C (77°F), pitch yeast. Ferment between 16 and 18°C (60–64°F) for one to two weeks. Bottle or keg and store for at least two weeks before serving. Serve at 6–8°C (42–46°F).

Belgian Trappist/abbey beer

Specifications
Colour: 16–24L
Bitterness: 24–30 IBU
Original gravity:
    1.075–1.085
Alc/vol 7–8%
Alc/wt 5.6–6.4%

Trappist beers and abbey beers are essentially the same thing, the only difference being where they are made. Belgian Trappist beers, by law, can only be brewed in one of the country's five Trappist monastery breweries. Abbey beers are often very similar in style, but can be brewed anywhere. These are usually strong beers but the characteristic they have in common is the unusual flavours imparted to them by the use of specialised yeasts. To a conventional brewer, they can taste infected, usually with a clove-like, spicy aroma and flavour, but it is this very characteristic that makes them drinkable by balancing out the enormous amount of fermentables used to brew them. This style (or range of styles) is the only one where the use of cane sugar is absolutely indispensable to keep the beers from becoming too thick, malty and cloying. If you can find Belgian-style candi sugar, that is the most ideal, but any form of cane sugar will do at a pinch. Hopping rates are not high and hop flavour and aroma restrained, so the hop variety used is not critical. This is a case, however, where the correct yeast simply must be used. This recipe is for a beer that would roughly equate with a dubbel in strength and colour, but you can vary it according to your taste. Since very large mashes become difficult to handle, some extract should be used in the formulation. This is not a beer to be brewed in a hurry. It will take months before it is ready to drink—but it should be worth the wait.

ALL-GRAIN

Metric (22.5 litres)		US (5 gal)
Grains/adjuncts		
5 kg	Pale malt	9 lb
300 g	Crystal malt (50L)	9 oz
200 g	Chocolate malt	6 oz
1 kg	Light dried malt extract	1.8 lb
500 g	Candi or brown sugar	15 oz
Hops		
28 g	NZ Hallertauer—full boil	0.8 oz
14 g	Fuggles—10 minutes	0.4 oz
Finings		
1 tsp	Irish moss	1 tsp
Yeast		
Belgian ale yeast		

Method
Mash and sparge the grains by one of the methods described in Chapter 13. Add the dried extract and sugar and boil the wort for 70 minutes, adding the Irish moss 30 minutes from the end, and the hops at intervals as directed. When cooled to below 20°C (68°F), pitch yeast. Ferment between 16 and 21°C (60–70°F) for two weeks. Transfer to a secondary fermenter or pressure barrel and store for at least two months before bottling. Store bottles for a further two months before serving. Serve at 6–8°C (42–46°F).

CAN KIT

1.8 kg	Belgian Ale can kit	4 lb
1 kg	Amber dried malt extract	2 lb
500 g	Malto-dextrin (corn syrup)	1 lb
14 g	Fuggles hop pellets	1/2 oz
Belgian ale yeast		

Method
Add contents of can to at least 2 litres (2 quarts) hot water in a large saucepan. Bring to the boil, stirring constantly to prevent sticking and burning, add dried extract, malto-dextrin and hop pellets, then simmer for 10 minutes. Pour into fermenter and top up with cold water plus ice if necessary. When cooled to below 25°C (77°F), pitch yeast. Ferment between 16 and 21°C for two weeks. Transfer to a secondary fermenter or pressure barrel and store for at least two months before bottling. Store bottles for a further two months before serving. Serve at 6–8°C (42–46°F).

18 Recipes for wheat beers

Bavarian weizen

Specifications
Colour: 3–8L
Bitterness: 10–16 IBU
Original gravity:
   1.048–1.055
Alc/vol 5–5.5%
Alc/wt 4–4.4%

Weizen is the most popular style of wheat beer in Germany and presumably in the world. Although it originated in Bavaria it is now brewed in many other parts of the country and available just about everywhere. One of the reasons for this growing popularity could be its lack of bitterness, for weizen is not a highly hopped beer. Its main characteristic is a quirky blend of phenolic-cum-fruity flavours that makes it a highly distinctive drink. It comes in two forms—a clear, filtered version known as kristall and the original unfiltered style, known nowadays as hefewiezen, from the German word *Hefe* meaning 'yeast'. This original style is cloudy because the yeast remains in suspension in the beer. The beer is made from a combination of barley and wheat malts in about 50:50 proportions, and top-fermented with one of the unique weizen yeasts.

ALL-GRAIN

Metric (22.5 litres)		US (5 gal)
Grains/adjuncts		
2.5 kg	Pale malt	4.5 lb
2.5 kg	Wheat malt	4.5 lb
Hops		
28 g	Hallertauer—full boil	0.9 oz
Finings		
1 tsp	Irish moss	1 tsp
Yeast		
Bavarian Weizen yeast		

Method
Mash and sparge the grains by one of the methods described in Chapter 13. Boil the wort for 70 minutes, adding the Irish moss 30 minutes from the end. When cooled to below 20°C (68°F), pitch yeast. Ferment between 16 and 18°C (60–64°F) for one to two weeks. Bottle or keg and leave for at least two weeks before serving. Serve at 6–8°C (42–46°F).

CAN KIT

1.8 kg	Weizen can kit	4 lb
500 g	Light dried malt extract	1 lb
500 g	Malto-dextrin (corn syrup)	1 lb
Bavarian weizen yeast		

Method

Add contents of can to at least 2 litres (2 quarts) hot water in a large saucepan. Bring to the boil, stirring constantly to prevent sticking and burning, add dried extract, and malto-dextrin, then simmer for 10 minutes. Pour into fermenter and top up with cold water plus ice if necessary. When cooled to below 25°C (77°F), pitch yeast. Ferment between 16 and 18°C (60–64°F) for one to two weeks. Bottle or keg and store for at least two weeks before serving. Serve at 6–8°C (42–46°F).

Belgian wit

The Belgians have a different approach from the Germans to making a wheat beer. Unfettered by any rules about what they can and cannot put into their beers, they often brew them from unmalted wheat and add exotic flavourings like bitter orange peel, ginger and coriander seed. *Wit* is Flemish for 'white' and the beer gets the designation because it is always cloudy with protein haze and yeast. The Belgians also do not go in for phenolic flavours so their wit yeasts produce a clean, rich flavour. It can be difficult for a home brewer to mash a large amount of unmalted wheat, but a fair replica of a wit can be made with the same grain formulation as a weizen, using 50:50 barley and wheat malts. This recipe calls for coriander seed, but you can experiment with other flavourings like ground ginger. Traditionally, Belgian wheat beer brewers have used hops more for their preserving effects than for their bittering power, so they have tended to use old, stale hops. We do not have to worry about preservation of the beer as it won't be passing through the hands of retailers, publicans and so on, so we can simply use low hopping rates and low-alpha varieties to get the delicate hop flavour and aroma we want.

Specifications

Colour: 3–5L

Bitterness: 12–20 IBU

Original gravity:
   1.048–1.055

Alc/vol 5–5.5%

Alc/wt 4–4.4%

ALL-GRAIN

Metric (22.5 litres)		US (5 gal)
Grains/adjuncts		
2.5 kg	Pale malt	4.5 lb
2.5 kg	Wheat malt	4.5 lb
Hops		
28 g	Hallertauer—full boil	0.9 oz
14 g	Saaz—10 minutes	0.4 oz
14 g	Saaz—at end	0.4 oz
14 g	Coriander seeds—at end	0.4 oz
Finings		
1 tsp	Irish moss	1 tsp
Yeast		
Belgian wit yeast		

Method

Mash and sparge the grains by one of the methods described in Chapter 13. Boil the wort for 70 minutes, adding the Irish moss 30 minutes from the end, the hops at intervals as directed, and the coriander seeds at the end. When cooled to below 20°C (68°F), pitch yeast. Ferment between 16 and 18°C (60–64°F) for one to two weeks. Bottle or keg and leave for at least two weeks before serving. Serve at 6–8°C (42–46°F).

CAN KIT

1.8k g	Belgian wit can kit	4 lb
500 g	Light dried malt extract	1 lb
500 g	Malto-dextrin (corn syrup)	1 lb
14 g	Saaz hop pellets	1/2 oz
Belgian wit yeast		

Method

Add contents of can to at least 2 litres (2 quarts) hot water in a large saucepan. Bring to the boil, stirring constantly to prevent sticking and burning, add dried extract and malto-dextrin, then simmer for 10 minutes. Add hop pellets, pour into fermenter and top up with cold water plus ice if necessary. When cooled to below 25°C (77°F), pitch yeast. Ferment between 16 and 18°C (60–64°F) for one to two weeks. Bottle or keg and store for at least two weeks before serving. Serve at 6–8°C (42–46°F).

Glossary of commonly used brewing terms

AAU	Alpha Acid Units—scale of measurement of hop bitterness
adjunct	any fermentable material other than malted barley
alpha acids	bittering substances found in hops
bottle-conditioning	carbonation of beer by secondary fermentation in bottle
bottom-fermenting	(of) yeast that falls to the bottom of the brew after fermentation
conditioning	carbonation of beer
dextrins	unfermentable sugars
dextrose	sugar derived from a grain, usually maize
diastase	combination of two enzymes that convert malt starches to sugars and dextrins
fermentables	materials which can be fermented by yeast
fermentation	process in which yeast converts sugars into alcohol and carbon dioxide
fermenter	vessel in which fermentation takes place
final gravity	specific gravity of wort after fermentation
finings	material (such as gelatine) added to beer to help it clear
flocculation	tendency of yeast to fall to the bottom of a brew
hop extracts	chemically derived extracts of hop acids and oils
hop oils	naturally occurring oils in hop cones—source of aroma
hopping	process of infusing hop bitterness, flavour and aroma into beer
hops	*Humulus lupulus* plant whose flowers (cones) are used for bittering beer
hot break	precipitation of proteins by boiling
late hopping	adding a proportion of hops late in the wort boil to preserve flavour and aroma
malt	grain treated in the malting process to convert starches into soluble form
malt extract	soluble sugars extracted from malted grains, usually condensed
malting	process of turning grain into malt
maltose	fermentable sugar derived from malted grain

mashing	process of extracting fermentable sugars from grain by steeping in hot water
original gravity	specific gravity of wort before fermentation
phenolic	medicinal flavour sometimes found in beer
pitch	adding yeast to a wort
primary fermentation	initial fermentation after yeast is pitched into a wort
racking	transfer of beer from one container to another
saccharification	conversion of starches in malted grain into sugars
secondary fermentation	second fermentation, either in a second fermenter or in bottle or keg
steep	to soak in liquid
top-fermenting	(of) yeast that rises to the top of the brew after fermentation
trub	protein material precipitated by hot break
tun	large vessel used in brewing
wort	solution of fermentable sugars in water
yeast	unicellular organism responsible for fermentation

Acknowledgments

This book would not exist without the generous help of many people all over the world. In Australia, Chuck Hahn and Geoff Scharer have been inspirations, while Traute Tuckfeld at the German National Tourist Office in Sydney and Hubert Cooleman at the Belgian Consulate have made many things possible. In Germany, priceless assistance was rendered by Stephan Barth of Joh. Barth & Sohn, Karl-Werner Adler of Löwenbräu, the Müller family of Pinkus Müller, Matthias Trum and Martin Knab of the Schlenkerla, Reinhard Krätsch of Sünner Brewery, Erich Dederichs of the Deutsche Brauer Bund, Dirk Schenzer of P. J. Früh, and many others too numerous to mention. In Belgium, Antoine Denooze introduced me to a new world of beer and many wonderful people, brewers and otherwise. In Britain, the Campaign for Real Ale, Young's Ram Rod Brewery, Fuller's and Bass gave valuable assistance, while Michael Jackson set me on the true path with a memorable night's pub crawl—and my family and friends helped me continue it. And no book that has anything to do with craft brewing could fail to acknowledge the work of Charlie Papazian, the man who made it all happen.

Bibliography

Daniels, Ray, 1996, *Designing Great Beers*, Brewers Publications, Boulder, Colorado.

Dornbusch, Horst D, 1997, *Prost! The Story of German Beer*, Siris Books, Boulder, Colorado.

Fix, George & Fix, Laurie, 1991, *Märzen, Oktoberfest, Vienna*, Brewers Publications, Boulder, Colorado.

Foster, Terry, 1990, *Pale Ale*, Brewers Publications, Boulder, Colorado.

— 1992, *Porter*, Brewers Publications, Boulder, Colorado.

Guinard, Jean-Xavier, 1990, *Lambic*, Brewers Publications, Boulder, Colorado.

Jackson, Michael, 1988, *The New World Guide to Beer*, Quarto, London.

— 1997, *Michael Jackson's Pocket Beer Book*, Mitchell Beazley, London.

Line, Dave, 1985, *The Big Book of Brewing*, Argus Books, Hemel Hempstead, UK.

— 1988, *Brewing Beers Like Those You Buy*, Argus Books, Hemel Hempstead, UK.

Miller, David, 1990, *Continental Pilsener*, Brewers Publications, Boulder, Colorado.

Papazian, Charlie, 1991, *The New Complete Joy of Home Brewing*, Avon Books, New York.

— 1994, *The Home Brewer's Companion*, Avon Books, New York.

Papazian, C., Meilgaard, M.C., Guinard J-X., et al, 1993, *Evaluating Beer*, Brewers Publications, Boulder, Colorado.

Rajotte, Pierre, 1992, *Belgian Ale*, Boulder, Brewers Publications, Boulder, Colorado.

Richman, Darryl, 1994, *Bock*, Brewers Publications, Boulder, Colorado.

Wheeler, Graham & Protz, Roger, 1993, *Brew Your Own Real Ale at Home*, CAMRA Books, St Albans, UK.

Index

Notes

Notes

Notes